FAITH IN CHRIST
OVER
FEAR OF CANCER

A Survivor's Testimony of Hope and Trust in God
Through the Battle Against Breast Cancer

Jestina Dennis-Fofana

FAITH IN CHRIST OVER FEAR OF CANCER. Copyright @ 2025. Jestina Dennis-Fofana. All rights reserved.

No part of this publication may be reproduced, stored in a retrieval system or transmitted in any form or by any means, electronic, mechanical, photocopying, recording or otherwise without the prior written permission of the author.

Published by:

Editor: Cleveland O. McLeish (Author C. Orville McLeish)

ISBN: 978-1-965635-55-1 (Paperback)

Scripture quotations marked "KJV" are taken from the Holy Bible, King James Version (Public Domain).

Scripture quotations marked (NIV) are taken from the Holy Bible, New International Version®, NIV®. Copyright © 1973, 1978, 1984 by Biblica, Inc.™ Used by permission of Zondervan. All rights reserved worldwide.

Scripture quotations marked "NKJV" are taken from the New King James Version. Copyright © 1982 by Thomas Nelson, Inc. Used by permission. All rights reserved. Bible text from the New King James Version® is not to be reproduced in copies or otherwise by any means except as permitted in writing by Thomas Nelson, Inc., Attn: Bible Rights and Permissions, P.O. Box 141000, Nashville, TN 37214-1000.

Scripture quotations marked "ESV" are from the ESV Bible® (The Holy Bible, English Standard Version®), copyright © 2001 by Crossway Bibles, a publishing ministry of Good News Publishers. Used by permission. All rights reserved.

This book is dedicated to all who have survived cancer or are currently battling cancer or any form of terminal illness.

I pray that my healing testimony will inspire you and strengthen your faith to maintain or receive the healing that God has made available to us through His Son, Jesus Christ. Regardless of the diagnosis you may have received, your healing is possible if you believe.

I am alive because I believed the Word of God. It worked for me, and it will work for you. God bless and keep you!

Acknowledgments

I extend my utmost gratitude to my "Team of Supernatural Doctors" – Dr. God Almighty, who sent His Word and healed me; Dr. Jesus Christ, who took my sins and sickness in His own body and healed me by His stripes; and Dr. Holy Spirit, who gives life to my mortal body. Heavenly Father, thank You for restoring my health and life. I am grateful!

My heartfelt appreciation to my loving husband and confidante, Boakai M. Fofana, Sr., whose unwavering support, love, prayers, and encouragement not only sustained me during the most difficult period of our lives but also afforded me the time needed to author this book. Thanks, my love.

Special thanks to my sister, personal doctor, and prayer partner, Dr. Estella Marlo Dennis, who supported me from the onset, encouraged me with scriptures and prayers during the most challenging times, and provided medical guidance to ensure that I did everything humanly possible to regain my health. Thank you, my "sister/doctor."

I extend my profound gratitude to my dearest aunt, my caregiver and prayer warrior, Louise M. Payne, who put her entire life on hold and travelled with me to another country for one year and stood by my side during all my appointments and treatments, while at the same time praying with me throughout my journey. God bless you, Tante!

To Mother Hadassah Abraham, who prayed with us and provided guidance and direction from the Lord when I needed it most, thank you, and may God bless you.

To Pastor Jerry Eze and the NSPPD (New Prophetic Season Prayer and Declarations) team, thank you a million times! The fire prayers and testimonies kept my faith alive and active, and today, cancer has been reversed by the power that raised Jesus from the dead. What they saw before, they did not see again.

Table of Contents

Acknowledgments v
Introduction 9
Chapter 1: My Story 13
Chapter 2: Jehovah Rapha – The Lord Our Healer 23
Chapter 3: God's Prescription and Medication for Healing . 35
Chapter 4: Whose Report Will You Believe and Agree With? 45
Chapter 5: Long Life Belongs to God's Children: Choose Life 55
Chapter 6: How to Use Your Faith to Beat Cancer and All Diseases 67
Chapter 7: Fear Not, The Lord Is With You 83
Chapter 8: Stand Firm 91
Chapter 9: Praise Is Our Weapon For Victory 105
Chapter 10: How To Keep Your Healing 113
Healing Scriptures 121
References 127

Introduction

The word "cancer" is one of the most dreaded words in the world today. It has become so powerful and terrifying that it is destroying the faith of God's children in His power to heal and deliver us from all infirmities, as written in His Word, the Bible. That is exactly what the devil wants, so that we can be kept in fear and bondage.

Cancer is like a death sentence, and almost everyone who receives a cancer diagnosis becomes overwhelmed with fear and begins to feel that life is over and that they are going to die. I felt that way myself at first, and it's natural to feel that way. I know and understand from experience. The fear of cancer is promoted everywhere, by the media, in movies, and in families because of the number of family members who have been lost to cancer, and by different organizations. I don't blame them; this disease has killed a lot of people. I don't think I have ever watched a movie where a character survived cancer; such movies always end tragically.

Yes, cancer is a terminal disease, but I believe the fear that comes with cancer is more deadly and causes a lot more deaths. Why do I say that? I believe that if cancer is treated with less fear and seen for what it is: an attack of the devil that can be defeated by faith in Jesus Christ and the Word of God, regardless of the diagnosis or stage, more and more people will experience God's healing from cancer. As a woman delivered and healed completely of stage three triple negative invasive breast cancer, I am here to tell you that Jesus Christ is bigger than cancer. He is the big C, and cancer is the little c—I heard this phrase from a pastor, and it stuck with me. 1 Peter 2:24 tells us that Jesus bore our sins in His own body on the cross, and by His stripes, we *were* healed. We are healed, as stated in Isaiah 53:4-5. All we need is to have faith in God and believe the truth of God's Word, which will set us free from cancer and all diseases.

The Bible says in Hebrews 13:8 that Jesus Christ is the same yesterday, and today and forever. Jesus is still healing today. This book is my way of encouraging anyone who is battling cancer or any form of terminal disease that you are not alone; God is with you. He is willing and able to heal you.

God heals in different ways. He heals some people supernaturally, while others may undergo a healing process with the help of doctors and medication, as I did. He also heals through natural means—using plants, herbs, and other elements. But no matter the healing method, God is the source of your healing, and the healing power of God is above doctors, medications, and any other form of healing. Jesus Christ is our healer and the Doctor over all doctors.

Faith in God is the key that releases healing. God's promises for your healing are written in His Word, the Bible. If you have faith in God and believe His Word concerning your healing, you will experience healing for whatever disease or infirmity you may be going through, no matter how long it takes. I urge you to have faith in God! Christ is bigger than cancer and all diseases. At the name of Jesus, cancer must bow. Say to yourself, like the woman with the issue of blood, *"If only I may touch the hem of His garment, I shall be made whole." (see Matthew 9:21-22)*. And indeed, she was made well according to her faith. *It was her faith in Jesus that made her well.* In the same way, your faith in Jesus Christ will make you well. Fear not, dear reader, only believe.

Faith in Christ will overcome cancer and all diseases every time. No matter what negative report you may have received, be it cancer, diabetes, heart disease, high blood pressure, etc., Jesus has already paid the price for our healing. By His stripes, we were healed (see 1 Peter 2:24). Do not give fear a bigger seat in your heart and life than Jesus. Christ is seated far above cancer and all diseases, and we are seated with Him. He already took all our diseases and infirmities. Matthew 8:17 tells us that *"He took our illnesses and bore our diseases." (ESV).*

No matter how many negative stories you may have heard or seen about the havoc cancer is causing in the world today, remember that the Bible says in Psalms 91:7 that, *"A thousand may fall at your side, ten thousand at your right hand, but it will not come near you." (ESV).* God has provided healing and deliverance for His children through

Jesus Christ, and anyone who calls on His name and believes in His Word will be saved.

The good news is that positive reports are rising daily of how God is healing people of cancer today. I have been healed, so I am living proof that God is healing cancer today. Will you believe God and receive your healing, or will you believe the deception of the devil and allow him to steal the healing and life your heavenly Father has already made available to you? The choice is yours, but I encourage you to choose life. I declare that you shall not die but live and declare the works of the Lord, as it is written in Psalm 118:17.

The Bible is the living Word of God; it is Spirit, and it is life. God is no respecter of persons. He healed me of stage three triple negative invasive carcinoma (breast cancer), and He can do the same for you. Have faith in God. All things are possible for those who believe (see Mark 9:23). I am living testimony! I pray that the Spirit of God will help you grow in your faith so you can accept and experience His love and healing, in Jesus' name. Amen.

Chapter 1

My Story

"I shall not die, but live, and declare the works of the Lord." (Psalm 118:17 – KJV).

I was diagnosed with invasive carcinoma, an aggressive kind of breast cancer, in May 2023 at the age of forty-five years. To say I was devastated is an understatement. I received the report from the doctor on a Friday evening, and I did not sleep a wink the entire night; I cried almost the whole night. Fear gripped me, and negative thoughts started to take over. I did not tell my husband immediately; instead, I began to pray and ask God for help.

As I cried and prayed, I began to reflect on all the storms that God had brought me through, and God's promises for my life as written in His Word. After a few hours of praying, I calmed down a bit and began to thank God for all His uncountable blessings. I was grateful for life; the fact that I was alive was a good place to start. I knew I couldn't overcome it on my own, so I turned to God and continued praying the entire night as I asked God to intervene. As I prayed, the Holy Spirit dropped in my spirit the scripture that says, *"I shall not die but live and declare the works of the Lord" (see Psalm 118:17)* and that *"life and death are in the power of the tongue" (see Proverbs 18:21).* I held on to God's Word and began to declare those scriptures over and over, reminding God of His promises for my life and health as I prayed.

By the morning hours, as I prayed, I heard a voice say, *"Don't worry. I've got you."* It sounded like someone whispered in my ear. I knew it was the Holy Spirit, and the Lord had heard and answered my prayer. At that moment, I felt a sense of peace and calm settle in my spirit. I just knew I was not going to die. I came to understand *"the peace of God that surpasses all understanding,"* which the apostle Paul talked about in Philippians 4:7. My faith in God's Word was my evidence that I was not going to die. I believed that God was going to heal me. And from there, my healing journey began.

I later broke the news to my husband, and he broke down in tears. I told him not to cry because nothing was going to happen to me. I was very calm, and seeing my faith and confidence in God also gave him the faith that I would be alright.

Although God had assured me through the Holy Spirit as I prayed, I knew I had to keep in His presence and continue to pray and trust Him. Fear was still trying to torment me, so I needed to keep feeding my faith with God's Word. I began to study God's promises regarding long life and healing, memorizing and meditating on several healing scriptures daily, and I also listened to healing messages. Faith comes by hearing the Word of God (see Romans 10:17), so as I spent time reading my Bible and listening to faith and healing messages, my faith began to grow.

Prior to my diagnosis, I was encouraged by my elder sister, Christine, to join an online prayer platform, NSPPD (New Season Prophetic Prayers and Declarations), which I joined. Little did I know that the enemy had sent some arrows at me, and God knew I would need strong faith to overcome all the attacks. Praise God for His love and mercy, as He made a way for me to join the prayer altar and build my faith before I received the negative report. Praying daily on the prayer line, I saw and heard healing testimonies of others, which increased my faith. I noticed that God heals people in various ways. Some people received instant miracles, while others experienced healing over time without any medical treatment, and some were healed through medical treatments: the same God, but different methods. But no matter the method, many people experienced healing through faith in God.

I knew I was not going to die because I had heard the voice of the Holy Spirit say clearly, *"Don't worry. I've got you,"* and also because of God's promises in His Word, which gave me assurance that I was not going to die but live and declare His works. However, I still wasn't seeing the healing manifest in my body. Instead, the lump seemed to be getting bigger. Every time I looked at the lump, fear would rise within me. However, I continued to declare that *"by His stripes, I am healed"* (see 1 Peter 2:24), *"I walk by faith and not by sight"* (see 2 Corinthians 5:7), and several other scriptures. I refused to give in to fear, and I continued my daily prayer on the NSPPD prayer line and continued to be encouraged by the many testimonies of people who were healed from cancer and other diseases.

A few weeks after my initial diagnosis, I travelled to a West African country to seek medical treatment. I found a good hospital and met the oncologist who ran some tests, confirmed the diagnosis, and provided me with the treatment plan. However, I was not led to take treatment at that hospital. I felt a heaviness in my spirit, so I returned home without taking the treatment and continued to pray and ask God to heal me supernaturally or lead me to the right hospital for my treatment. I depended on God to direct my path, and I thank Him for leading me to where He wanted me to go because the Lord orders the steps of the righteous; He knows the end from the beginning. I returned home and continued to pray and put my trust in God.

The lump began to grow rapidly. Every time I looked at the lump, which had become huge and visible, fear would rise up. One day, as I explained to my younger sister, Estella, how the lump looked and made me feel, she prayed with me and urged me to stop allowing the devil to use fear to delay my healing. She encouraged me to look at the lump and

FAITH IN CHRIST OVER FEAR OF CANCER

speak God's Word over it. After this, I stopped allowing my body to tell me I wasn't healed. I became bold, and my faith in Christ became bigger than my fear of cancer. Instead of describing my situation or describing how I felt, I kept declaring God's Word concerning my healing. I chose life, and I spoke life every day (see Proverbs 18:21).

Instead of crying when I looked at the lump, I would look in the mirror and speak to it. I began to speak God's Word over my body and commanded it to align with the Word of God. I cursed the spirit of cancer and declared that I was not going to die but live. I continued to speak life over myself every day. It reached a point where fear almost disappeared. I say "almost" because I had to constantly battle with the spirit of fear, but my faith helped me overcome it. I began to walk by faith and not by sight. The lump was still there, but my reaction to it had changed. During the waiting period, I also changed my diet. I eliminated alcohol and sugar, added more vegetables and fruits, and began to eat healthier. Throughout this period, I continually renewed my mind with healing scriptures, spoke the Word, and remained connected to the NSPPD Fire Altar: my online prayer group. My faith in Christ continued to grow, and I continued to trust God for my healing.

If you or a loved one is in a similar situation, I want to encourage you to have faith. Fear can delay your healing because when you fear, you begin to doubt, and when you doubt, you become unstable. As stated in James 1:7, an unstable or double-minded person should not expect to receive anything from God. Thank God that He is merciful, and even in the midst of doubt, He still answers, because He knows that we believe in our hearts. You build up your faith by hearing the Word of God. Keep reading and listening to the Word of God concerning healing. Memorize healing scriptures in this book and others in the Bible, and declare them at least three times a day—that's what I did—and at many other times. God will come through for you.

Eventually, I was led to seek treatment at a hospital in South Africa. Through God's divine intervention, and with the support of my husband, Boakai M. Fofana Sr., my sister, Dr. Estella Marlo Dennis, and my aunt and prayer partner, Mrs. Louise Payne, who accompanied me and stood with me throughout my treatment period, I left to seek medical care at a hospital in South Africa, where I met a wonderful team of professionals and doctors who had faith in God. In fact, one of the doctors told me that she's more than a medical doctor; she's a servant of God, and the Lord sent her to me to encourage me and let me know that I was going to be healed. This carried my faith to a new level!

My Oncologist was also a woman of faith who shared with me that God had healed her miraculously when she was a teenager. I have come to know and understand that God's plans are always better than ours. Continue to trust Him, regardless of your circumstances. He will come through for you.

So, five months after the diagnosis, I began medical treatment. It took me five months because I was praying and asking for God's guidance; I also wanted to travel out of Africa for treatment, but God had other plans. Moreover, I didn't want to go through chemotherapy. I was healthy prior to the cancer diagnosis, and I heard how harsh chemotherapy was, so I was afraid to go through with it. I kept praying for God to take the cancer away and heal me supernaturally, but His plans are not our plans, neither are His ways our ways. His grace is sufficient to guide us through; we must keep trusting Him.

Note: *I do not advise anyone diagnosed with cancer to wait five months before starting treatment. The sooner you start your treatment, the better. However, I encourage you to pray and ask for God's guidance.*

God led me to the right place, and He was with me throughout my healing journey. My relationship with God has become stronger. My faith in Christ overcame the fear of cancer.

My Treatment Journey

After going through all the tests, I met with the doctor for my results. I kept praying and declaring throughout the different tests, CT scan, biopsy, blood tests, etc, that I was healed. I continued to declare healing scriptures and believe in God for my healing. Later, as I sat in the doctor's office, she began to review my results with me. As I listened to her, I began to reject all the negative reports she gave me, not audibly, but in my spirit. The doctor told me that it was triple negative, stage 3 invasive breast cancer, and she proceeded to give me details of the treatment plan: surgery, chemotherapy, radiation. My Aunt Louise was with me, and she was also praying the whole time. As I listened to the doctor, I continued to reject the negative report in my heart and thanked God for my healing. I was not afraid because, for me, the first miracle was that even though the lump was big and the cancer had spread to three of my lymph nodes, the cancer had not spread to any other part of my body; it had remained in the area where the lump and the lymph nodes were. I knew that my God was working!

I was then scheduled for surgery. However, a few days later, the doctor called and informed me that the treatment plan had changed. They had decided to start with chemotherapy instead to reduce the lump before surgery. At that point, I began to battle with the spirit of fear again. I was afraid to proceed with chemotherapy; I had read about all the negative effects of chemo, so naturally, I was afraid. Again, we went to God in prayer, and while praying, the Holy Spirit revealed to one of my prayer partners that I should go ahead with chemotherapy, that it was not going to harm me; it would rather be used to heal me. After this confirmation, I began chemotherapy. I prayed and asked God for guidance and direction for every step of my healing journey. And He always led me.

Chemotherapy is a hard journey, but I am grateful to God that the effects for me were much less than I expected because God was with me. I was not hospitalized for one day throughout the treatment, except for two days after my surgery. Every time I went for chemo, I asked God to send His angels ahead. When they brought the drugs, I prayed, spoke to it, and declared that it had become the blood of Jesus and that all side effects were canceled, in Jesus' name. Even the doctors were amazed at my response to the treatments. They kept asking what I was doing to keep looking lively and *"bright,"* as the doctors described it. I told them that it was God's grace because *"What God can not do does not exist."* Even the lab technician who took my blood weekly could not believe that I was on chemotherapy. She asked me if I was taking any other herbal drugs, and I said no, but I was taking God's medicine. God is my strength.

Jesus Christ is the same yesterday, today, and forever! I am convinced that chemotherapy alone would not have worked as well as it did if I had not relied on God for my healing because I know that *"It is better to trust in the Lord than to put confidence in man." (Psalm 118.8 – KJV).*

I completed sixteen cycles of chemotherapy. Throughout the treatments, we continued to pray, declare, and believe God's Word. After completing my chemotherapy treatments, I did the surgery. And, yes, my God came through for me. The lymph nodes and tissues removed from my breast did not have any trace of cancer. Glory be to God! The Oncologist insisted that I do radiation, so I did, but again, God kept me through, and I completed radiation without any issues. God is faithful. For me, it was a journey, but through it all, I continued to lean on Jesus. I held on to the written promises I share in this book.

I know that healing is God's will, and He wants all of His children to prosper and be in good health (see 3 John 2). Keep trusting God; He will not fail you. He is Jehovah Rapha, the Lord our healer. My life is a testimony that God is our Healer.

Chapter 2

Jehovah Rapha – The Lord Our Healer

"...I am the Lord that healeth thee." (Exodus 15:26 - KJV).

His name is Jehovah Rapha: the Lord, our healer. The Hebrew word for "health" is *Rapha*, meaning to heal, cure, or restore. God is Jehovah Rapha, our healer. He wants us to be well. He wishes, above all, that we prosper and be healthy, even as our souls prosper. Sometimes, we are deceived into believing that God has afflicted us with cancer or other diseases. We begin to blame God and ask, *"Why me?"* I also asked that question.

Some people accept sickness and disease as God's way of punishing them for the bad things they might have done, or assume that it is God's will. I know that it is NOT God's will because God's will for us is written in His Word, and that does not include sickness. 1 Peter 2:24 tells us that "He himself bore our sins in his body on the tree, that we might die to sin and live to righteousness. *By His wounds you have been healed." (NIV)*. If sickness is God's will, then Jesus suffered and died in vain. But we know that He did not die in vain; that is why we know that we are healed, in Jesus' name!

The truth is that sickness is an oppression of the devil, but *"God anointed Jesus of Nazareth with the Holy Spirit and with power, who went about doing good and healing all who were oppressed by the devil, for God was with Him." (Acts 10:38 – NKJV)*. God does not make us sick; the devil does. Satan is the thief who has come to steal, kill, and destroy. Jesus is the healer who has given us abundant life, which includes salvation, health, healing, and all good things (see John 10:10). God is a good God; He does not punish us with sickness. Every time God brought sickness in the Old Testament, it was a curse. However, praise God that Jesus has redeemed us from the curse of the law, which includes sin and sickness (see Galatians 3:13). Sin allows sickness because it separates us from God. Jesus, the lamb of God, has taken away our sins by His blood, and we are no longer separated from God as long as we believe and accept Jesus as our Lord and Savior.

When we confess our sins, ask God's forgiveness, and rely on Him, He will heal and deliver us according to His Word. We have been saved by grace through faith, not by works. God is a loving and forgiving Father. Ask Him right now to forgive your sins and deliver you from all oppression of the enemy, and let the blood of Jesus cleanse you from all unrighteousness.

FAITH IN CHRIST OVER FEAR OF CANCER

The devil has deceived many Christians into believing that supernatural healing is outdated. Instead of trusting God, some people rely solely on natural medicine. I am not against hospitals; I was treated at a hospital, and I took medicine. However, I have come to realize that medications sometimes fail, but God never fails. God wants us healed and well. Even if you are on medication, take God's medicine first. His Word is His medicine. What I like about God's medicine is that it gives you strength and hope, even when your body is saying something else. As one minister puts it, *"Healing starts within your spirit (God's Word is Spirit and it is life), then enters your soul (your mind, will, and emotions) and your mind tells your body what your spirit already knows, that you are healed."* That is why you need to nourish your spirit and soul daily with the Word of God, and your body will eventually follow suit. You will gradually begin to walk by faith and not by sight.

Strong faith takes time to build, but all we need is a mustard-seed faith to move mountains (see John 17:20). Spend time reading and listening to God's Word because faith comes by hearing. If you are on medication, pray over it before taking it. Ask God to use it to heal you. God will meet you wherever you are in your faith. The key is to trust Him for your healing. Jesus is the Doctor of all doctors. His Word is health/medicine to our flesh.

Once I settled this truth in my heart—the fact that God is my healer, healing is His will, and Jesus already took my disease [cancer] in His own body on calvary—my prayer became,

"Lord Jesus, I thank You for taking cancer away from my body because according to Your written Word in Matthew 8:17, You took all my afflictions and carried all my sickness so I don't have to bear cancer in my body. I believe that I am healed according to Your Word, and I thank You that I have been healed from breast cancer, in Jesus' name. I pray for Your grace and strength to continue holding on to Your Word and keeping my heart and eyes on You, in Jesus' name. Amen." I did not pray, *"Oh, Lord, if it is Your will, please heal me."* God's will is written in the Bible, and His Word says, *"I am healed,"* and that is the same for everyone who believes. By His stripes, you are healed!

Matthew 9:35 tells us, *"Then Jesus went about all the cities and villages, teaching in their synagogues, preaching the gospel of the kingdom, and healing every sickness and every disease among the people." (NKJV). "Jesus Christ is the same yesterday, and today and forever." (Hebrews 13:8 – KJV).* The same Jesus who healed in the Bible is the same Jesus who healed me. I was healed from stage 3 invasive breast cancer through faith in God's written Word, so I know that God is still healing today. He does not change; He is our healer forever. Have faith in God; anything is possible if you believe.

God is the Healer; Look to Him, Not the Method

God heals in different ways. Jesus performed several healing miracles, but the methods were different. Let's look at a few of the healings. Matthew 8:2-3 tells us about the leper who was healed.

FAITH IN CHRIST OVER FEAR OF CANCER

> *"And, behold, there came a leper and worshipped him, saying, Lord, if thou wilt, thou canst make me clean. And Jesus put forth his hand, and touched him, saying, I will; be thou clean. And immediately his leprosy was cleansed." (KJV).*

Notice that Jesus reached out and touched the leper, and he was healed **immediately.** The leper believed that Jesus could heal him; Jesus answered his faith with a touch, and immediately, he was healed.

In the case of the Centurion's servant, Jesus did not see or touch him; He spoke the Word, and the servant was healed.

> Matthew 8:8, *"The centurion answered and said, "Lord, I am not worthy that you should come under my roof. But only speak a Word and my servant will be healed." (NKJV).*

> Matthew 8:13, *"Then Jesus said to the centurion, go your way; and as you have believed so let it be done for you. And his servant was healed that same hour." (NKJV).*

The centurion believed that a word from Jesus was sufficient to heal his servant, and he received what he believed for. He received it according to his faith.

The woman with the issue of blood in Matthew 9:20-22 reached out in faith and touched the hem of Jesus' garment, and she was instantly healed. She believed that if she touched Jesus' garment, she would receive her healing. As she believed, she received her healing according to her faith.

John 9:1-7 talks about the healing of the man born blind. In this instance, Jesus spat on the ground, made clay with the saliva, and anointed the eyes of the blind man. Then, he told him to go and wash in the pool of Siloam. So, the blind man went and washed in the pool and came back seeing. In this healing, Jesus instructed the blind man to go and do something. His healing manifested after he washed in the pool.

In the case of the demon-possessed boy, the disciples tried to cast out the unclean spirit, but they could not. As soon as Jesus arrived, He commanded the spirit of deafness and dumbness to come out of the boy; it came out, and he was healed. Jesus later told His disciples that they could not cast the spirit out because *"this kind does not go out except by prayer and fasting."* (see Mark 9:17-29).

Another method of healing is seen in Acts 19:11-12, where *"God worked unusual miracles by the hands of Paul, so that even handkerchiefs or aprons were brought from his body to the sick, and the diseases left them, and the evil spirits went out of them." (NKJV)*. I could go on and on, but I think you get my point. The same healer, different methods of healing.

Some people believe that when you go to the hospital, you are not believing God. I have come to realize that God will not refuse to heal anyone because he/she choose to seek medical intervention. He can use the doctors and medicine to heal you. He can also heal supernaturally without any medication. It all depends on your faith. God has given every believer a measure of faith, but we have to feed our faith for it to grow and become strong. Our heavenly Father is a good God and a merciful savior; He will meet you wherever your faith is.

If you have faith in supernatural healing, go for it; God will come through for you. If you want to undergo chemotherapy or any other medical treatment, go for it. If you choose to take herbal medicine, do so with guidance from the Lord through prayer and the Word of God. I believe that doctors, medication, herbs, and other methods are all points of contact for our healing; God is the ultimate healer. Pastor Oral Roberts described the point of contact as *"any point where your faith contacts God's power. Any point, whether it is the spoken word, the hem of Jesus' garment, the laying on of hands, or anything else."* God uses many different methods to heal. The key is to have faith and believe God for your healing, knowing that He is our healer. He says, *"For I am the God who heals you." (see Exodus 15:26).* Don't get fixated on the method like I was before God directed my path through prayer. Look to Jehovah Rapha, the Lord your Healer, not the method.

Same God, Two Different Methods of Healing

Following the breast cancer diagnosis, I decided to confide in my aunt, who is a woman of faith and the "prayer warrior" in my family. Up to this point, only my husband, Boakai, and my sister, Estella, knew of the cancer diagnosis. I did not want crying and sadness from well-meaning loved ones because that was going to feed my fear, and I needed to feed my faith. I needed people with the same level of faith I had or more. When I told my aunt, she encouraged me by sharing her story of how God had healed her supernaturally several months prior to my diagnosis. This is her story.

God Healed Me Supernaturally (Lousie P)

I woke up one morning with pain in my right breast. I felt my breast and noticed there were two lumps. I could not believe it, so I called my granddaughter and asked her to check my breast and tell me if she noticed anything. She confirmed that she felt two lumps in my breast as well. At that point, I began to panic. I was shocked and afraid at the same time, but I began to encourage myself, and after a while, I became a little bit calmer.

A few days later, I went to the hospital. The doctor did a physical check on my breast and confirmed that there were two lumps. I was scheduled to return for further tests, including a mammogram. By this time, the pain in my breast had intensified to the point that I could not lie down on my stomach. I had to lie on my left side or on my back.

On the day of my appointment, I got ready, but as I was about to leave for the hospital, I heard a voice. I knew it was the Holy Spirit saying, *"Am I not able to heal you?"* At that point, I fell on the floor of my room in tears and began to ask God to heal me. I decided against going to the hospital and put my hope and trust in God instead. I believed God was willing and able to heal me; after that, I began to fast and pray.

I am on an online midnight prayer altar, Alpha Hour, and our pastor usually prays over the point of contact water, which members drink and use for various sicknesses and afflictions. I had heard several testimonies of miracles and healings from members who used the point of contact water and holy communion.

These testimonies helped increase my faith, so I got a box of 0.5-liter bottles of water and holy communion. I began my daily fasting and midnight prayers. I drank the point of contact water, did holy communion, and used them both as lotion. I rubbed them on my body twice daily. At first, I was constantly checking and realized that the lumps were still there. Fear started creeping in again, but I continued to pray and ask God for forgiveness, mercy, and healing.

I continued to pray, but the lumps remained after a week of fasting and prayer. At this point, I decided to stop checking myself and keep my eyes on Jesus. He is my healer. He said that by His stripes, I am healed. He had told me that He is able to heal me. I decided to take God at His Word.

There were days when I cried and lamented to God. I asked Him to intervene because I did not have any money to pay for treatment. I had no one to depend on except Him, so I relied on Him to heal me according to His Word. At this point, I had stopped checking if the lump was still there. One day, about two weeks after I started the fast and prayer, I went to lie down and decided to lie on my stomach. To my astonishment, I felt no pain. I got up and lay down again on my stomach and on my breast, and I didn't feel any pain. I then checked my breast, but there was no lump. The two lumps had completely vanished! God did it! He healed me completely without any medication! I began to dance and glorify God! That was the end of it. That was over two years ago, and since then, God has kept me, and I know that affliction will not arise a second time. Praise God! Jesus healed me.

God Healed me Through Chemotherapy, Surgery, and Radiation (Jestina F)

As you know from my story, God used doctors and medicine to heal me. He uses different methods for healing His children. After hearing my aunt's testimony, as well as several other testimonies of supernatural healings on the NSPPD Prayer Altar, I also wanted God to heal me supernaturally, without chemotherapy, surgery, or radiation. The "Fire Altar" kept my faith alive and my prayer life active as I joined every weekday and on Sundays. But the truth is, although I wanted supernatural healing, I was in a serious battle with the spirit of fear. I was on a roller-coaster of faith and fear, and where there is fear, doubt is also present—one day I wanted supernatural healing, the next day I was asking God if I should do chemotherapy. Eventually, the word came through Pastor Jerry Eze, Lead Pastor of NSPPD online prayer platform, that triple negative breast cancer had been reversed, and what the doctors saw before, they were not going to see again. Additionally, God, in His mercy, gave a word to one of my prayer partners that I should go ahead with chemotherapy and that it was not going to harm me; instead, it was going to help me.

God knew the measure of faith I had, so He met me where I was. I believed the word that came through prayers and went ahead with the medical treatment: chemotherapy, surgery, and radiation. However, I did not rely solely on the medications; God is my healer, and I relied on Him and took God's medicine (the written Word of God) daily. God met me where my faith was, and I came out without any complications from the drugs because I trusted Him to heal me.

God heals in different ways. Some people experience instant healing miracles, while others are healed within weeks. There are those who undergo a healing process similar to the one I did. Only God knows how long it will take before you see your healing manifest. The key is to keep believing, confessing your healing, and praising God until your body cooperates and manifests your healing. As Rev. Kenneth Hagen said in one of his teachings, *"That's why you are a believer; keep believing!"* You will experience healing for whatever disease or infirmity you may be going through right now if you continue to stand on God's Word. God is faithful; His Word will never return to Him void. It is essential that you follow God's prescription and take His medication in addition to any other natural remedies you may choose to use. I took God's medicine every day–I still do. Let me share with you how I applied God's medicine.

Chapter 3

God's Prescription and Medication for Healing

> *"My son, give attention to my words; Incline your ear to my sayings. Do not let them depart from your eyes; Keep them in the midst of your heart; For they are life to those who find them, and health to all their flesh." (Proverbs 4:20-22 – NKJV).*

During my healing journey, I read many books on faith and healing, and one of them was Rev. Kenneth Hagen's book, "God's Medicine." After reading the book, I began to apply God's medicine. Let me share with you how I took God's medicine. Before taking natural medicine, a prescription is required. God also has a prescription for His medicine. God's written prescription is found in Proverbs 4:20-23.

God's prescription requires that *you give attention to His written Word and incline your ear to His sayings;* this means that you should listen carefully and focus on what the Word is telling you without being distracted by negative reports or anything that contradicts the Bible. *Do not let the Word depart from your eyes*; read the Bible and keep your eyes on the written promises for your healing instead of looking at your body, symptoms, or the medical report. *Keep them in the midst of your heart;* meditate on the Word and believe it in your heart; allow the Word—the double-edged sword—to penetrate your spirit through faith. The Word is Spirit, and it is life; as you read, listen, meditate, and confess the Word daily, it will restore your life and health.

How I Applied God's Medicine

"My son give attention to My Word."

I set aside a specific time each day to give my attention to the Word of God. Early in the morning, before getting out of bed, I read my Bible, especially the healing scriptures. I also had prayer time at 3:00 am, 7:00 am, and 7:00 pm. I would also read a few healing scriptures, meditate on them, and pray before going to sleep. I would spend fifteen minutes to an hour.

Read the healing scriptures in this book and other healing scriptures in the Bible. Set aside God's meeting time, whether it's five minutes or one hour or more. Be intentional and set aside a specific time to spend in God's Word. Just as the doctor gives a prescription and says, *"Take this pill twice a day, morning and evening, or every 12 hours or so,"* that's the same way you have to set aside time to take God's medicine if you want your healing to manifest. The more time you spend in the Word, the stronger your faith to believe and receive your healing. You have 24 hours in a day. How much of those 24 hours can you spend with God? You decide. God is a loving Father; He won't judge you. He just wants you to have time to spend with Him and get to know and trust Him for your healing.

"Incline your ears to My sayings."

I would read the scriptures silently and also read them out loud. As you hear the Word, it sinks in and helps build your faith. There are many times when I have asked the Holy Spirit to reveal the Word to me and help me understand the scriptures. Ask the Holy Spirit to reveal the scriptures to you because all scriptures were inspired by the Holy Spirit. Faith comes by hearing and hearing by the Word of God. Listening to teachings on healing will also help to build your faith. I'm always reading and listening to healing scriptures and teachings. I also listen to healing testimonies, and I can tell you that God is healing many people today of various diseases. Hearing these testimonies will help build up your faith. There are several online.

"Let it not depart from your eyes."

I have healing scriptures on my wardrobe right in front of my bed. As soon as I wake up, I review some of those verses and begin my day with faith in God's Word for health and healing. I also printed several healing scriptures and had a copy in my bag, and I posted some on the cabinet in my office. I kept my eyes and heart filled with the Word of God daily. This helped me to stand firm in my faith and believe that I was going to live and see my healing manifest.

You can print out healing scriptures and post them on your wall, mirror, or stick-on pads where you can view and read them regularly. Keep your eyes on God's Word rather than on your body or symptoms. Choose to believe God's written report instead of the doctor's report. Remember that we walk by faith and not by sight. This is something I will continue to do because the enemy is always attacking, so we must remain sober and vigilant.

> *"Keep it in the midst of your heart."*

I kept the Word in my heart by meditating on the scriptures and allowing them to sink in. I would read two or three healing scriptures, close my eyes, and review them in my mind, allowing them to sink into my heart. For instance, I would meditate on 1 Peter 2:24, *"who Himself bore our sins in His own body on the tree, that we, having died to sins, might live for righteousness–by whose stripes you were healed." (NKJV)*. I would keep repeating this to myself:

> *Jesus already carried my sin in His body. I died to sin through His death on the cross. Every beating He received, the shame, disgrace, and agony were all for my salvation and healing. By His stripes, I was healed, and so I am healed! Thank You, Lord, that I am healed.*

FAITH IN CHRIST OVER FEAR OF CANCER

I would close my eyes and imagine being healed and receiving my new medical report—my *praise report*, as I called it. Whenever I had negative thoughts, I intentionally began to read the healing scriptures and declare them over my life. I visualized what my healing would look like; I began planning things I would do after I completed my treatment. I would praise God for healing, even when I had not yet seen the physical evidence in my body. That is how I keep the Word in my heart.

I suggest that you take time to read some healing scriptures and meditate on them instead of thinking about the cancer or disease in your body. I'm not saying this is easy because it is easier to believe what we see and feel. This is why we must continue to read God's Word to strengthen our faith. Whenever you have negative thoughts, intentionally begin to read healing scriptures, repeat them to yourself, and declare them over your life. Visualize what your healing will look like and the things you will do when your healing manifests in your body. See your new medical report! Praise God for healing you, even if you have not yet seen the full manifestation of your healing in your body. That's what faith is about: believing what you have not seen and trusting that God will do what He says.

Jesus told Jarius not to be afraid, even after he was informed that his daughter had died. He said to Jarius, *"Do not be afraid; only believe, and she will be made well." (Luke 8:50 NKJV)*. Meditate on the healing scriptures, and like Jarius, do not be afraid; only believe. No matter how hopeless your situation may seem, God's Word has the power to reverse it! Don't get tired because the devil doesn't get tired. Even if you feel tired, do it anyway. Don't let your body defeat you. Ask the Holy Spirit for strength.

> *"For they are life to those who find them, and health to all their flesh."*

Jesus said, *"The Words that I speak to you are spirit, and they are life." (John 6:63 – NKJV)*. God's Word is life! I was healed of stage 3 breast cancer, so I am a living testimony that God's Word is life and health. Have faith in the Word of God. He is Jehovah Rapha, the Lord our healer. He wishes, above all, that you prosper and be in good health even as your soul prospers. Nothing is impossible with God. Have faith, and you will be healed.

In addition to hearing the Word, keeping it before your eyes and in your heart, you need to speak the Word. Speak the Word to the mountain (cancer, heart disease, diabetes, or whatever mountain is standing in the way of your blessing from God). Command that mountain of cancer or whatever affliction that is attacking your body to be removed, in Jesus' name! Your own words must align with God's Word.

You must confess what you believe; your mouth must confess what your heart believes. Life and death are in the power of the tongue. Say to the mountain (cancer, diabetes, heart disease, etc.):

FAITH IN CHRIST OVER FEAR OF CANCER

"Be removed, in Jesus' name."

God has given us the authority to speak to any mountain in our lives. You can't believe that you are healed, but confess that you are sick and hopeless. You cannot own the sickness by saying, *"I have this disease. I am not well. I don't know what to do."* etc. You should say, *"The doctor said I have this, but I know that I am healed, in Jesus' name."* That is what I did, and it helped increase my faith; the devil also heard and knew that I was holding on to God's Word.

Declare that you are healed, as it is written. Speak to your body and use the scriptures to manifest your healing. Discourage any form of negativity from "well-meaning" family and friends. No *"Poor thing,"* or *"You know you are sick, so you can't do this or that,"* etc. What they don't realize is that these words increase your fears instead of your faith. So, keep speaking health and healing over your life. Don't join any "pity party." It only weakens your faith. Be strong in the Lord and in the power of His might. He will see you through. Nothing is impossible with God.

Keep taking it to the Lord in prayer. Be persistent. God sees and hears you. He will hasten His Word to perform it. Continue to send your prayers to Him as often as possible. When you are sitting, lying down, or wherever you are, remain in God's presence and pray without ceasing. I had a prayer schedule: three times a day. I would go to a quiet place to pray. Sometimes in the room, sometimes in the bathroom; anywhere. I'd just speak to God and remind Him of His promises, pour out my heart to Him, and thank Him for listening and coming through for me.

You have to follow God's prescription and take His medicine if you want to see healing manifest in your life. Also, bear in mind that there is a time for sowing and a time for reaping, so be patient and stand firm—having done all to stand, keep standing until you see the results. Trust that God is not a man to lie. What He has said, He will surely do! Fear not; only believe!

Natural medicine works overtime if you follow the doctor's prescription and take the dosage as prescribed. The length of time you have to take the medicine varies depending on the ailment and your body's reaction to the medicine. The key is to take the medicine consistently and in the right dose. Likewise, for God's medicine to be effective, you must take it consistently and in the correct dosage. You can even double the dose if the symptoms persist. That is the advantage of God's medicine: only good side effects! However, don't forget to consult your Team of Supernatural Doctors every step of the way so that your doctor on call, the Holy Spirit, can guide you. He is on call 24/7.

I followed God's prescription, which I'm sharing with you, and took God's medicine. It worked for me, and it will work for you. God is no respecter of persons. Today, I am healed from stage 3 invasive breast cancer and other infirmities. It is the result of taking God's medicine. He is healing so many people today. Fear not; only believe! Nothing is impossible with God.

I suggest that you join a community of believers to pray and build your faith. Joining the NSPPD Fire Altar and praying every weekday at the altar has helped improve my prayer life and deepen my faith. This is important to help you grow in faith. You can be healed, even if you do not join a community, but it helps to strengthen your faith.

In addition to my personal time with God and my local church, I am also part of an online prayer ministry, where God is performing miracles and helping people overcome cancer. Being on the prayer line and listening to other people's testimonies helped strengthen my faith in God and receive my healing. I urge you to connect to a community of believers to help you remain grounded in the things of God. Ask the Holy Spirit to guide you to the right platform; He will!

Chapter 4

Whose Report Will You Believe and Agree With?

"Who hath believed our report? and to whom is the arm of the Lord revealed?" (Isaiah 53:1 - KJV).

When I received the diagnosis of breast cancer, my initial reaction was to cry and feel sorry for myself. As I began to think about my husband and children, my mother, and my entire family, and what would happen, I started asking God, *"Why me?"* and so on. To say I was devastated is an understatement. But thank God for His Word. I knew a few Bible verses about healing and long life, and I held on to those scriptures. I began to reject the medical report and chose to agree with God's Word for my health, healing, and long life instead. I refused to have any "pity party." I decided to believe God's promises for my life and began to declare them daily over my life. I told myself over and over that I was not going to die but live and declare the works of the Lord as written in Psalm 118:17. I kept repeating that to myself until I knew, with confidence, that I was not going to die because God is not a man that He should lie. I believe that Jesus died for my sins. I had accepted Him as my Savior since I was a child. It was time to accept Him as my healer, as well, because it is written in God's Word that by His stripes, I have been healed. I held on to those promises and refused to contradict them. I came in complete agreement with God's Word.

Remember that the thief comes to steal, kill, and destroy (see John 10:10). The sickness attacking your body is meant to steal your peace, time, finances, faith, and ultimately, your life. However, the good news is that Jesus came to give you abundant life; He has already paid the price for your healing, having borne all your infirmities and carried your sickness (see Matthew 8:17). By His stripes, you were healed (see 1 Peter 2:24). So, whose report will you believe? The report written by the medical doctor, created by God, or the report written by God in His Word? Thank God for medical doctors; they are doing their jobs and helping, and I appreciate them. However, Dr. Jesus has the final say. Will you agree with your body, symptoms, and feelings that are contrary to what is written in God's Word?

Yes, the doctors may be reporting what they see, and your body may be hurting or showing symptoms of the disease, and you may be feeling sick, but as believers in Christ Jesus, we do not walk by what we see; we walk by what the Word of God says. *For we walk by faith, not by sight.* (2 Corinthians 5:7 - NKJV). God's Word says that by His stripes, you were healed! God's report says, *"I am the Lord that heals you." (Exodus 15:26 - NKJV)*. God's report says, *"I shall not die but live and declare the works of the Lord" (see Psalm 118:17)*. God's report says, *"With long life will I satisfy you and show you my salvation" (see Psalm 91:16)*. God's report says, *"He will give life to your mortal body through His Spirit who dwells in you (see Romans 8:11)*.

Can two walk together unless they are agreed? (see Amos 3:3). Are you agreeing with God or with the devil? There is no middle ground. You have to choose who you are going to walk with. Remember that one is a thief and the father of lies, and the other is your Savior and Healer, your loving Father who can never lie, for it is impossible for God to lie. He has said that His Word will never return to Him void but will accomplish the purpose for which it was sent (see Isaiah 55:11). I urge you to come into agreement with God's Word.

There is power in agreement. When you come into agreement with God's Word, you empower the Word to work for you, but when you agree with the medical report or your symptoms, you empower the enemy to work against you. Whatever you agree with will become your reality. No matter what your medical report says, declare that you reject it and believe God's report instead. As the doctor gives you all the diagnoses, remember and declare in your heart that you are healed in Jesus' name, as it is written. As soon as you are alone, begin to declare it out loud. Say to that mountain of sickness, *"Be removed from my body, in Jesus' name."*

Abraham believed God; he agreed with God that his offspring would be as numerous as the stars, even though he was already old and had no children (see Genesis 15:5-6). His name was changed from Abram to Abraham, even before he became a father. He agreed with the Word of God; he made a choice to see himself as God saw him: the father of many nations. There was no evidence that he was the father of many nations, yet he called himself Abraham (meaning *"father of many nations"*) instead of Abram. He did not let his weakness, age, or body hinder him from being in agreement with the Lord. He remained in agreement with God and eventually received the promise.

Eve, on the other hand, listened to the deception of the devil and came out of agreement with God and into agreement with the lie the enemy told her. Adam also bought into this deception, and both of them came out of agreement with God and into agreement with the devil. This agreement worked against them and led to the fall of mankind (see Genesis 3:1-6). Be careful that you don't allow the devil to deceive you through fear because you have received a negative report. That report is not the truth; God's Word is the truth. His Word will never return to Him void. He says in Jeremiah 30:17, *"I will restore health to you and heal you of your wounds." (Jeremiah 30:17).* Remain in agreement with the Word of God, and you will see your healing manifest.

Jesus was in total agreement with God. He said in John 8:29, *"And He who sent Me is with Me. The Father has not left*

Me alone, for I always do those things that please Him." (NKJV). And in John 10:30, He says, *"I and my Father are one." (KJV).* His agreement with the Father gave Him power, through the Holy Spirit (see Acts 10:38), and He *"went about doing good and healing all who were oppressed by the devil, for God was with Him."* He restored to us what the thief (the devil) stole (See John 10:10): salvation, health, healing, peace, prosperity, and every good gift that God has given to us. He won the victory for us. We are no longer slaves to sin and fear. Jesus already died in our place. He has redeemed us from the curse of sin; that curse includes any sickness, be it cancer, diabetes, hypertension, heart disease, and ALL diseases. Jesus became a curse for us. He took our sins in His own body (see 1 Peter 2:24). He Himself took our infirmities and bore our diseases (see Matthew 8:17), so we don't have to take them again.

Jesus already took cancer and all diseases away, praise God! We have been bought with the precious blood of the Lamb, the pure Lamb of God. You don't have to be sick because Jesus paid the price for your healing. You are an overcomer because *"He who is in you is greater than he who is in the world." (1 John 4:4 – NKJV).* Come into agreement with God's Word, and it will work for you. This is an agreement with the Creator of all things. He never goes back on His Word. It always works; you just need to agree with Him and stay in agreement, no matter what your five senses or the medical report tell you. I am telling you that God can be trusted. He is faithful. I am a witness, and I'm testifying to His love, mercy, loving-kindness, and faithfulness.

Know the Word to Agree With the Word

To agree with the Word of God, you have to know the Word. Spend time reading your Bible, and get to know God through His Word. The Word is a lamp unto your feet and a light unto your path (see Psalm 119:105). You cannot agree with what you don't know, or at least, you shouldn't agree with what you don't know. The Bible says, *"but the people who know their God shall be strong and carry out great exploits." (Daniel 11:32 – NKJV). We gain* strength from the Word, and with the Word, you will defeat fear, sickness, and all afflictions. Find healing scriptures and read and meditate on them every day. When you know the truth of God's Word, the truth will set you free from sickness and diseases and anything that is contrary to the Word of God.

I came into agreement with God's report—His written Word—and I drafted a new report in faith. It eventually became my reality. Below is what I wrote. If you like, you can write yours and insert your name where I have mine.

Good Health Report

To: Jestina Dennis Fofana
Date: August 19, 2023

"It is better to trust in the Lord than to put confidence in man." (Psalm 118.8 – KJV).

With God, nothing is impossible. Fear not, only believe. What they saw before, they will not see it again, in Jesus' name. Amen. What my God can not do does not exist!

Dear Jestina:

Having reviewed your body from head to toe and completed full tests of all your cells, organs, tissues, muscles, blood vessels, and every part of your body, we (the Team of Supernatural Doctors – Dr. God Almighty, Dr. Jesus Christ, and Dr. Holy Spirit), who formed you in your mother's womb, and know every part of you, hereby inform you that you are cancer free and 100% healthy. The spirit of cancer has been evicted from your breast and your body to the glory of God! We also want to inform you that all cells in your body are functioning normally as God intended them to function. Dr. God Almighty sent His Word and healed your disease. He removed cancer and all sickness from your body. He has forgiven all your iniquities and healed all your diseases (see Exodus 15:26, Psalm 103, Exodus 23:25-26). Dr. Jesus bore in His own body all your sins and diseases and healed you by His stripes. He redeemed you from the curse of the law (cancer and all diseases) by becoming a curse for you (see 1 Peter 2:24, Galatians 3:13). Dr. Holy Spirit dwells within you and has given life to your mortal body (see Romans 8:11).

Dr. Jesus already healed you from all infirmities over 2,000 years ago when He bore in His body all your sickness and healed you by His stripes. He paid the price for your healing. Therefore, Jestina, you are 100% healed! To God be the glory!

Additionally, Dr. Jesus defeated death and the grave, and all diseases bowed at the Name of Jesus, the Name that is above all names. Therefore, you are now healed in the name of Jesus. You shall not die but live to declare the works of the Lord in the land of the living. God has said it; therefore, it is done. Amen.

Jestina, the blood of Jesus was shed for you and brought you back into the presence of God Almighty, where there is no sin, sickness, or disease but righteousness, peace, and joy in the Holy Spirit.

The hand of the Lord is not too short to save you, Jestina. Dr. God Almighty, your heavenly Father, reached down and saved you. He has healed you by the same power that raised Jesus from the dead, the power that dwells within you, Jestina—the power of the Holy Spirit, His life-giving spirit.

Congratulations, Jestina! Jesus has set you free. The Holy Spirit is with you to ensure that you remain in God's presence and never return to your old life; you now walk in divine health. All sicknesses and diseases have been removed from your body, mind, and soul by your heavenly Father, Dr. God Almighty. Affliction (cancer) will not rise up a second time because the blood of Jesus has made an utter end of it, according to Nahum 2:9.

CONGRATULATIONS, Jestina Dennis Fofana!

You are healed on this 19th day of August 2023. You were healed by the Team of Supernatural Doctors: Dr. God Almighty, Dr. Jesus Christ, and Dr. Holy Spirit. Affliction (cancer) shall not rise up a second time. The blood of Jesus has made an utter end of it (see Nahum 2:9). Go in peace and share your testimony of God's love and healing. Jesus loves you!

Signed: The Team of Supernatural Doctors: Dr. God Almighty, Dr. Jesus Christ, and Dr. Holy Spirit.

I held on to this date as the date I was healed because Mark 11:24 tells us that whatever we pray for, we should believe that we have received it, and it will be ours. Our prayers are answered when we pray. We must continue to believe until we see our answer manifest in the natural world.

I thanked God that I was healed on August 19, 2023. Even when I was still undergoing chemotherapy in 2024, I continued to call forth my healing and declare that I was healed in August 2023. And my healing manifested eventually. That's how faith works. It is evidence of things not seen. You don't need faith for what you already have.

You apply faith to get what you are believing God for. And God never fails. He will come through for you. He did it for me, and He will do it for you as well. Have faith!

Chapter 5

Long Life Belongs to God's Children: Choose Life

> *"I call heaven and earth as witnesses today against you, that I have set before you life and death, blessing and cursing; therefore, choose life, that both you and your descendants may live." (Deuteronomy 30:19 – NKJV).*

Regardless of the circumstances we face in life, we always have a choice. God gave us that right from the beginning when mankind was created. We are faced with different choices every day. This is no different when we are battling disease or affliction. We can choose to stand on the Word of God and choose life or give in to the deceptions of the enemy. God cannot make the choice for us; He has already made healing and long life available through the blood of the New Covenant, the blood of Jesus Christ. God's plan is for us to live long, healthy lives and not die prematurely. He wants us to live the full number of our days and fulfil His purpose for our lives. He promised to satisfy us with long life and show us His salvation (see Psalm

91:16). He gave man one hundred and twenty years (see Genesis 6:3). Jesus said all things are possible if you believe (see Mark 9:23). If it is written in the Bible, it is God's will. Choose life by reading, believing, and confessing God's Word for your healing every day until you see it manifest in your body.

As I stated earlier, the first scripture that the Holy Spirit spoke to my heart right after I received the cancer diagnosis was Psalm 118:17, *"I shall not die, but live, and declare the works of the Lord." (KJV)*. This verse literally saved my life. I held on to this verse and declared it every day until I believed it without a doubt. I later added several other healing scriptures to my daily declarations, but this verse was, and still is, the foundation for my health and healing. I chose to believe God, and I put all my hope and trust in His Word. I chose to see the blessings I already had, not the sickness. Every morning, after I praised God for a new day and expressed my gratitude for all He had done for me, I declared, *"I shall not die but live and declare the works of the Lord."* The Word of God works. I am a living testimony!

God is no respecter of persons. If it worked for me, it will work for you. You must take hold of God's Word and let it take over. Rely on Jesus. He will come through for you. However, you must do your part. Put the Word to work. Read it, meditate on it, believe it in your heart, declare it; the Word is alive, powerful, and sharper than any two-edged sword (see Hebrews 4:12). Use it to cut off cancer and all sickness and affliction from the root. Say to that mountain of sickness:

> *"In the name of Jesus, I curse you, cancer, from your root to your seed, and I command you to come out of my body right now, in the name of Jesus. Thank You, Lord, that I am healed. I shall not die but live and declare the works of the Lord, in Jesus' name, Amen."*

You have to choose life and speak life, as it is written in the Bible. God knows that the thief will do all he can to steal, kill, and destroy, so He provided us with the double-edged sword—His Word—to defeat the enemy.

A lot of Christians are destroyed because they lack knowledge of God's Word. 2 Timothy 2:15 tells us to study to show ourselves approved unto God. Jesus overcame Satan's temptations with the Word (see Matthew 4:4-7). To every temptation, He responded, *"It is written."* When you are tempted by fear of death because of cancer or any other sickness, tell the devil:

> *"It is written, I shall not die but live and declare the works of the Lord. I shall build houses and inhabit them; I shall plant vineyards and eat their fruit. I shall not build, and another inhabit; I shall not plant, and another eat. I shall enjoy the work of my hands (see Isaiah 65:21-22)."*

This is a promise from my heavenly Father, and you need to stand on His written Word, which will never fail.

I listened to a minister of the gospel share a story about a young man he had prayed for. He said that this man was in his early twenties and was in the intensive care unit (ICU) in a coma and on the verge of death. The doctors had given up on him and told his family that he would take his last breath at any moment. The pastor prayed for the young man, and as he was about to leave, the Holy Spirit prompted him to instruct the wife of the man, who was sitting at her husband's bedside, to declare Psalm 118:17 over her husband. She was instructed to say, *"Lord, I thank You for healing my husband. I thank You that he shall not die but live and declare Your works."* She had to keep on saying it over and over all day, every day, until his situation changed. And she obeyed. She kept on saying over her husband, who was in a coma, *"Lord, I thank You for healing my husband. I thank You that he shall not die but live and declare Your works."* She kept on repeating it several times a day, every day, and little by little, the almost-dead man started to recover. She continued to declare until he had fully recovered, after two weeks, to the amazement of the doctors. The Word of God works. It is Spirit, and it is life.

I don't know which report you have received, but whatever that report says, you must reject it and choose to believe God's written report for your life. You must make a choice. Deuteronomy 30:19 states, *"I call heaven and earth as witnesses today against you, that I have set before you life and death, blessing and cursing; therefore, choose life, that both you and your descendants may live."* Life and blessing go together; death and cursing go together.

God has promised to satisfy us with a long life, but we have to choose to live. You choose life by believing in the one and only true God and Jesus Christ, whom He sent, and allowing the Holy Spirit to help you yield and obey God's Word. You need to live and declare that your God is bigger than cancer and all diseases and afflictions. Let the devil know that God has given you the power to trample over all the power of the enemy (see Luke 10:19), and he can't steal the life and healing that Jesus suffered and died to give you. You need to live to fulfill your purpose. You need to live for your family and loved ones. You need to live and enjoy the fruit of your labor.

You choose life by surrendering your life to Jesus and presenting your body as a living sacrifice to God.

We have all sinned and fallen short of God's glory (see Romans 3:23). That is why Jesus came and died for us. We are not perfect, but we can live holy lives through Jesus. He is our righteousness. Do not think you can live for God on your own. If you think that, you are bound to remain in sin. Thank God that we are *"justified freely by His grace that is in Christ Jesus" (see Romans 3:24)*, so by God's grace, through faith in Jesus, we can surrender to God and allow the Holy Spirit to help us live according to God's commandments.

Jesus said that the greatest commandment is love; not the law, but love. When you love the Lord your God with all your heart, with all your soul, with all your mind, and with all your strength, and love your neighbor as yourself (see Mark 12:30-31), there is no way the devil can harm you. Where there is love, fear and every form of malice and negativity is cast out. God is love, so where there is love for God and love for others, God is present, and no disease can survive. We must have the mindset that God's love for us is too great for sickness to survive in our bodies. God so loved us that He sent His only begotten son to save us. Jesus Christ came to save us from the oppression of the devil; by His stripes, we are healed.

Apostle Paul says in Romans 12:1, *"I beseech you therefore, brethren, by the mercies of God, that ye present your bodies a living sacrifice, holy acceptable to God, which is your reasonable service." (KJV).* The Bible says in 1 Corinthians 6:19 that your body, my body, is the temple of the Holy Spirit, whom we have from God and not our own.

God gives life to our mortal bodies through His Holy Spirit who dwells in us (see Romans 8:11). Therefore, no sickness, including cancer, can survive in our bodies, which is God's temple. When we accept Jesus as our Lord and Savior, our spirit is born again, and the Holy Spirit helps us present our bodies to God, which is a "reasonable service." Reasonable because all God wants is for us to surrender completely to Him, allow Him to be the Lord of our lives, and ask Him to take control of every aspect of our lives. It's not because He wants to boss us around, but so that He can live in us through His Holy Spirit and keep us safe from the evil one.

When we present our bodies as a living sacrifice, we say no to things that we want because we know that they may not be good for us. Instead of satisfying our own desires and cravings, we seek those things that are pleasing to God. When we live right, the enemy cannot destroy us because God will protect us if we continue to trust and rely on Him. Besides, when we live right, we experience peace and joy that the world cannot understand. When the enemy attacks us with sickness and afflictions, we stand firm and trust in God because we know that our bodies are not our own, and He will restore our health. Therefore, we continue to believe that we are healed according to the Word of God, and His Word never fails. I am a living testimony!

You choose life by thinking about life not death.

Think positive thoughts about your life and health. Do not allow your mind to entertain negative thoughts. Keep your thoughts focused on the good things that God has done for you and the good things you are trusting God to do in your life. As long as you are breathing, you have something to be grateful for. Romans 12:2 says, *"And be not conformed to this world: but be ye transformed by the renewing of your mind, that ye may prove what is that good, and acceptable, and perfect, will of God." (KJV)*. The Word of God has the power to renew your mind from fear to faith, from negativity to positivity. If you feed fear with negative thoughts, it will grow and lead to negative outcomes. However, if you feed your faith with the Word, your mind will be transformed and renewed to think thoughts that are aligned with the Word. You have to choose whether to feed faith or fear.

What we think about when we are going through a life-threatening diagnosis is crucial. We need to feed on the Word of God so that our thoughts are focused on health, healing, and God's promises. *"For as he (a person) thinks in his heart, so is he." (Proverbs 23:7).* Your thoughts have the power to change your outcome, so be intentional about renewing your mind from sickness to health, from lack to abundance, from hopeless to very hopeful, and from fear to faith. Whenever you hear that voice of fear and negativity whispering in your ear, and you start imagining all sorts of bad things, immediately counter that voice with a Bible verse on faith and healing or whatever you are believing God for. Use the double-edged sword for *"Casting down imaginations, and every high thing that exalteth itself against the knowledge of God and bringing into captivity every thought to the obedience of Christ;" (2 Corinthians 10:5 - KJV).* Align your thoughts with the Word.

You choose life by speaking life.

Words are powerful. Words are carriers; they carry life, health, healing, love, confidence, hate, death, etc. Words can create good or evil, life or death. That is why we need to be mindful of the words we use. If children grow up in a home where they are told regularly that they are stupid, they will eventually begin to believe it and think of themselves as stupid. On the other hand, if a child is constantly told that he/she is smart, the child begins to believe it and acts accordingly. Even as an adult, if you wear a suit and one or more people tell you that your suit looks nice, you feel more confident because you believe it suits you well. With a negative word, you can cut someone to pieces, emotionally or mentally. Similarly, with a positive word, you can build confidence and give life.

Words are powerful. The world was created by the Word of God. In Genesis 1, we see that God spoke, and the heavens, the earth, and everything in them were created. We were created in the image and likeness of God. His creative power lives in us, and that includes the power of life and death, as determined by the words we speak. Proverbs 18:21 tells us that *"Death and life are in the power of the tongue: and they that love it shall eat the fruit thereof." (KJV)*. What seeds are you planting with your words? Seeds of death or seeds of life? The fruit you eat is determined by the seeds you plant. Orange seeds will bear orange, guava seeds will bear guava, seeds of death will produce death, and seeds of life will produce life. Sow seeds of life every day with the words you speak. Declare that you are healed in Jesus' name.

Jesus said in Mark 11:23, *"For assuredly, I say to you, whoever says to this mountain, 'Be removed and cast into the sea,' and does not doubt in his heart, but believes that those things he says will be done, he will have whatever he says." (NKJV)*. As stated before, when I was diagnosed with breast cancer, I was devastated. But praise God for His medicine—His written Word—because I held on to God's Word and declared and confessed it several times a day. I chose to live! I chose to believe God's report about my life, as stated in His Word. There were times when negative thoughts arose. I would see a report or hear about someone who died of cancer, and the fear of death would grip me. But as soon as the fear began, I also began declaring God's Word over my life to quickly replace fear with faith. I also guarded what I allowed my eyes to see and ears to hear. I mostly watched or listened to faith and healing programs.

I thanked God continuously for blessing me with a long life and revealing His salvation, as described in Psalm 91:16. Trusting God and choosing life means choosing daily to believe what the Word of God says about your life and healing, regardless of your symptoms. Stand firm in your faith, and you will see the salvation of the Lord. You will see your healing manifest in your body. Your life is important to God. He wants you to live. That is why Jesus came to give us life, and not just any life, but a more abundant life. You need to believe that and align your words with the Word of God.

Don't let yourself or anyone else speak negatively over your life. Throughout my healing journey, I always declared that I was well and doing great, even when I didn't feel that way. Every time a friend or family member sent me a text or called to check on me, I always responded that I was doing well or doing better, thanks to God's grace. I did not encourage any conversation that was contrary to the Word. I refused to say words that described how I felt or what the medical report said. In fact, I was careful not to tell too many people about the diagnosis. Every time you repeat the diagnosis or your symptoms, you agree with it, and it becomes more real to you. I was not in denial; I was speaking the truth in faith, according to God's written Word. In my case, I realized that when I told my loved ones, they started to panic and cry, which built fear in me instead of faith. So, after I got the same reaction of tears and fear from a few family members, I decided that was it. I was not going to tell anyone or mention the doctor's report again. Instead, I was going to declare what the Word says, and I told God that my family and friends would hear my testimony, not the negative report. And that's exactly what happened.

I had to stay in God's presence and keep out all negativity from some well-meaning friends and family members because I realized that I needed to hear faith words instead of fear words. Words have the power to give life or death, so be very intentional about speaking words of life and healing instead of words of sickness and death. I was also intentional about my self-talk. I spoke the Word to myself and constantly reminded myself of all the storms the Lord had brought me through, praising God for all He was doing at that moment and for all that I trusted Him to do for me in the future. I remained grateful for life and thanked God constantly. Guard your self-talk; align your words with the Word of God and choose life by speaking life!

Chapter 6

How to Use Your Faith to Beat Cancer and All Diseases

> *Hebrews 11:1, 6, "Now faith is the substance of things hoped for, the evidence of things not seen. But without faith it is impossible to please Him, for he who comes to God must believe that He is, and that He is a rewarder of those who diligently seek Him." (NKJV).*

Feed Your Faith

God has given all believers a measure of faith. However, for your faith to grow, you have to feed it. Faith is like a seed; it needs to be planted and watered daily to grow. This isn't done in one day; faith needs to be fed daily. If not, it will get weak. For our faith in God to reach a point where we believe in healing, we must keep our eyes and ears open to God's Word daily. Faith comes by hearing the Word of God. The more knowledge you have of God's Word, the stronger your faith will grow.

Jesus said in Matthew 4:4, *"It is written, "Man shall not live by bread alone, but by every word that proceeds from the mouth of God." (NKJV).* Just as the body needs physical food to survive, your faith needs spiritual food—the Word of God—to thrive. If you starve your physical body, it will become weak. Similarly, if you starve your faith, it will become weak. Faith is our weapon to quench all the fiery darts (cancer and all diseases and infirmities) of the enemy and give us victory to overcome cancer and all diseases. Feed your faith every day so it can be strong enough to quench all the fiery darts of the enemy. Here is a point to remember: Isaiah 55:11 tells us that God's Word will never return to Him void; it will accomplish that which God pleases, and it will prosper in the thing *for which He sent it.* The thing you need when you are sick is healing. You need God's Word for your healing. To have faith for healing, keep your eyes and heart on healing scriptures. It is not the time to read about prosperity, sin, marriage, etc. Those are all good, but read and confess the Word of healing first, and then you can later focus on other areas of need. You need your health and healing to be able to achieve all other things.

When you are sick, what you need is healing, not a new job or wealth or anything else. Let the Word of God prosper for you in healing. As you read and listen to healing scriptures, ask the Holy Spirit to reveal His truth to you. Meditate (memorize it, reflect on it, mutter it to yourself, think about it) on God's promises until it sinks into your spirit. Take two or three Bible verses on healing at a time—Isaiah 53:5, Matthew 8:17, and 1 Peter 2:24 are excellent scriptures to meditate on for healing. God's Word will never return to Him void; it will accomplish what He has promised. Feed your faith with God's Word, and trust that He will come through for you. What you believe is what you will receive. Faith works.

Cultivate Unwavering Faith

Hebrews 10:23 states that we should hold fast to the confession of our hope without wavering because He who promised is faithful. This means you should remain firm and consistent in your faith in God's written Word and continue to confess your healing no matter what you see, hear, or feel. You continue to trust that God is a loving and faithful Father, and His Word will not return to Him void. So, you decide to keep believing and declaring until you see your healing manifest. Know that Jesus is in the boat with you, and the Holy Spirit dwells within you, giving life to your mortal body. You have been bought with a price, the blood of Jesus, so sickness has no right to your body; it is trespassing on God's property because your body is the temple of the Holy Spirit—God's Spirit. Don't forget that. Hold on!

Abraham had unwavering faith. Hebrews 11:17-19 states that *"By faith Abraham, when he was tested, offered up Isaac, and he who had received the promises offered up his only begotten son, of whom it was said, 'In Isaac your seed shall be called,' concluding that God was able to raise him up, even from the dead, from which he also received him in a figurative sense." (NKJV)*. When God told him to offer up Isaac, the promised son, he did not waver. Instead, he believed that God was able to raise Isaac from the dead if necessary. Romans 4:20 tells us that *"He (Abraham) did not waver at the promise of God through unbelief, but was strengthened in faith, giving glory to God." (NKJV).* Abraham trusted God completely, and God came through.

Your faith may waver at times, especially if you are in pain and your healing hasn't manifested in your body. But God is merciful, so in those times, ask Jesus to take over. Jesus never fails. Don't stay in that place because if you do, the enemy will take advantage of your weakness, and you may begin to focus on your feelings and the medical report instead of God's Word, and that may delay your healing. You have a two-edged sword in your hand. Keep using it to cut off all cancer cells from the root and curse it so that, like the fig tree that Jesus cursed in Matthew 21:18-19, it will wither and die. The Word is Spirit, and it is life!

Faith calls the things which are not as though they are.

> *Romans 4:17b, "...God, who quickeneth (gives life to) the dead, and calleth those things which be not as though they were." (KJV – emphasis mine).*

I urge you again not to focus on your body, symptoms, or feelings; rather, look to what God says about your life, health, and healing. He is the God who calls things that have not yet come into existence as though they exist. As a child of God, created in His image and likeness, you can also call those things which are not as though they are. Do not give room to fear, even if you hear negative news of other people with similar diseases, because no matter how many may fall at your side, it will not come near you (see Psalm 91:7). Your faith in God will deliver you from every fear and give you the assurance that you will not die, but live and declare the works of the Lord (see Psalm 118:17). Faith is the evidence of things not seen. The flesh sees before believing; faith, on the other hand, believes before seeing. God's Word is the evidence of what you have not seen. And God cannot lie, so trust Him.

After I began treatment, the lump on my breast started to shrink; however, there was still some heaviness and anomalies, and my blood test showed that the cancer markers were still high. Discouragement and fear wanted to set in, but I rebuked them, and instead of focusing on my body and the negative report, I began to focus on God's Word.

Every morning, the first thing I would do was wake up and thank God for my healing. I would declare:

> *"Lord, I thank You for forgiving all my iniquities and healing all my diseases, according to Psalm 103. You are Jehovah Rapha, my healer, and I thank You for sending Your Word and healing me of cancer. Jesus, I thank You for taking all my infirmities and bearing all my diseases, including cancer, according to Matthew 8:17. I agree with Your Word and declare that I shall not die but live and testify of Your love*

> *and healing power. I declare that by the power and the blood of Jesus Christ, I am healed and set free from cancer. Body, you are already healed, so in the name of Jesus, I command you to align with the Word of God! I walk by faith and not by sight. Lord, I thank You for healing me and making me whole, in Jesus' name. Amen."*

I made these declarations (not in the exact words every time, but similar) several times a day and at night before going to sleep. My body and report did not change immediately, but I kept declaring that I was healed and thanking God for my healing, regardless of how I was feeling or what my symptoms were. Whenever doubt tried to step in, I began declaring God's Word and praising God for my healing. I kept calling things that were not as though they existed, and eventually, my healing manifested, to God be the glory! He is faithful.

Call your healing into manifestation by declaring you are already healed before you have any physical evidence of your healing. Keep telling yourself that you are healed because it is written, and because God said so, your body must cooperate. God is Jehovah Rapha. He says, *"... For I am the Lord who heals you." (Exodus 15:26),* and Jesus demonstrated this throughout His ministry on earth. He healed all who were sick and oppressed by the devil (see Acts 10:38). Keep holding on to your faith and confessing your healing. Don't say what you see or feel in your body; speak what the Word says. By His stripes, you were healed, and you are healed (see 1 Peter 2:24). Begin to praise God for your healing. It is done! Have faith, and you will not die but live and testify of God's healing and faithfulness in your life.

Have Faith in the Name of Jesus

> *"Wherefore God also hath highly exalted him, and given him a name which is above every name: That at the name of Jesus every knee should bow, of things in heaven, and things in earth, and things under the earth; and that every tongue should confess that Jesus Christ is Lord, to the glory of God the Father." (Philippians 2:9-11 – KJV).*

There is power in the name of Jesus, and Jesus Himself has given everyone who believes in Him the authority to use His name in every situation. Cancer and all diseases must bow at the name of Jesus. On our own, we have no power to defeat sickness because sin gives Satan access to oppress us with sickness, but Jesus died in our place, took all our diseases in His own body, and restored our health and life. Jesus has given every believer the privilege to ask for anything in His name (see John 14:14). If we ask according to His will, He will hear us, and healing is part of God's will. He is our healer.

Jesus has given every believer the legal authority, the power of attorney, as lawyers would say, to use His name in every situation, including casting out devils and laying hands on the sick. However, we need to ensure that we confess our sins and ask God's forgiveness (for we all have sinned and fall short of the glory of God) and submit our lives to God. Satan is the accuser of the brethren, so he will bring up our sins and shortcomings to deceive us into thinking we do not qualify to use Jesus' name. And, yes, we are sinners, and on our own, we do not qualify, but we are not depending on our own righteousness. We are the righteousness of God in Christ Jesus, and He has qualified us and given us the authority to use His name to cast out cancer and all diseases and oppression of the devil (see Mark 16:17-18). There is now no condemnation to those who are in Christ Jesus (see Romans 8:1). Jesus has set us free from the law of sin and death. We are the righteousness of God, through the finished work of Christ on the cross, not by our own works. Therefore, stand firm in the righteousness of Christ by accepting God's forgiveness and exercising the authority we have through the name of Jesus.

When God created man, He gave authority to Adam and Eve in the garden to have dominion over all the earth, but Satan deceived them, and they handed the authority over to him. Every day, we are faced with the same deception from the devil. These temptations come in many forms, including fear, doubt about God's Word, and doubt about our authority to use the name of Jesus, among others. We hear this voice asking, *"Are you really healed? Can't you see your body and the symptoms; do you feel healed? Don't you think the doctor's report is more real because you can see it? Jesus has power and authority, but you are a sinner. Do you have authority?"* Instead of being deceived like Adam and Eve, resist the enemy and begin to stand on your authority in the name of Jesus. Jesus reclaimed what the devil had stolen (health, healing, peace, long life, prosperity, etc.) through His death on the cross. He has come to give us a more abundant life! Begin to declare that you are already healed in the name of Jesus. Begin to bind cancer and all diseases from operating against you, in the name of Jesus—the name that is above all names, in heaven, on earth, and under the earth. Cancer and all diseases must bow at the mention of the name of Jesus. Stand on God's Word because Jesus has given you authority to overcome all the powers of the enemy (see Luke 10:19).

Command that cancer, or whatever disease that is attacking your body, to leave in the name of Jesus. Say:

> *"Cancer, in the name of Jesus, I command you to leave my body now. In the name of Jesus, I curse you, cancer, from your root to your seed. I speak death over every cancer cell that is attacking my body. In the name of Jesus Christ, come out now and never return to my body. Thank You, Jesus, for my healing. I stand on Your Word and receive my healing. To You be all the glory. Amen."*

Have Faith in the Blood of Jesus

> *"And according to the law almost all things are purified with blood, and without shedding of blood there is no remission." (Hebrews 9:22 – NKJV).*

God is not a man to lie, nor the son of man to change His mind. Once He has spoken, He cannot go contrary to His Word. He said that without the shedding of blood, there is no remission or forgiveness of sin. Therefore, Jesus had to shed His blood to establish the new covenant, by which all believers are purified from sin through the blood of Jesus. In the old covenant, the blood of animals was used continuously, but with Jesus, the mediator of the new covenant, His blood was shed once and for all, so that we can walk boldly to the throne of grace and ask for forgiveness through the blood of Jesus, the pure Lamb of God. We can boldly declare that we are healed because of the blood of Jesus. His blood washes us from our sins and makes us righteous to stand before our heavenly Father. According to 1 John 1:7, *"But if we walk in the light as He is in the light, we have fellowship with one another, and the blood of Jesus Christ His son cleanses us from all sin." (NKJV).*

We no longer have to go through a priest as was done in the old covenant, but we can go directly to God in prayer because of the blood of Jesus and declare that the devil cannot harm us with sickness because of the blood of Jesus that was shed for our sins.

We overcome cancer and all attacks of the enemy by the blood of the lamb. The Bible tells us in Revelation 12:11, *"And they overcame him by the blood of the Lamb and by the word of their testimony..." (NKJV).* Cover yourself with the blood of Jesus.

You can purchase communion wine, pray over it (or ask your pastor to pray over it, if you prefer), rub it on the affected area, and then drink some. As you drink the communion, declare that the blood is flushing away all sickness and disease from your body, in the name of Jesus Christ of Nazareth. If you don't have communion wine, you can use water as a symbol of the blood or simply declare and speak the blood over your body. Also, speak the blood of Jesus over your family. That is what I do every morning: I declare that my family is covered from the crown of our heads to the soles of our feet in the blood of Jesus. I call out their names, and through faith, I cover them with the blood of Jesus. I declare that the blood of Jesus protects us from all harm, danger, and all the arrows of the enemy.

Jesus has redeemed us from the curse of the law by becoming a curse for us when He hung on the cross and shed His blood to deliver us from sin and sickness. He made us partakers of the blessings of Abraham (see Galatians 3:13-14). We are blessed through Christ and partakers of all the blessings of Deuteronomy 28:1-14. Therefore, Jesus has redeemed us from every form of sickness under the law. Sickness is a curse because of sin and disobedience, but Jesus Christ paid the price for our sins by bearing our sins in His own body on the cross. We are saved and healed by grace through faith. However, sin gives the devil access to afflict us with sicknesses and diseases; that is why we need to repent and let the blood of Jesus cleanse us from sin and heal us.

Isaiah 53:5 tells us that by the stripes (or wounds) of Jesus, we are healed. The blood of Jesus was shed through the wounds that He received from the beatings, scorching, smacking, piercing, crown of thorns pushed on His head, and the crucifixion on the cross. Christ went through all the shame and pain to redeem us from sin and heal us from all sickness and diseases. Because of the blood, we have forgiveness of sins and healing from all sickness and diseases.

Hebrews 12:24 tells us that the blood of Jesus speaks for us. The blood speaks forgiveness. If we confess our sins, He is faithful and just to forgive us our sins and to cleanse us from all unrighteousness. No matter what sin you have committed, if you repent, the blood of Jesus will cleanse you. Don't let the accuser, the devil, tell you otherwise. Jesus' blood speaks forgiveness, salvation, and healing.

Hebrews 9:24 tells us that Christ is now in heaven in the presence of God for us. He is our high priest, interceding for us. The blood intercedes whenever the accuser of the brethren (the devil) brings charges of sin against us. The blood intercedes and sets us free!

Jesus shed His blood for us. He has already paid the price for healing. All we have to do is agree with the Word and the healing power in the blood.

FAITH IN CHRIST OVER FEAR OF CANCER

Have Faith in God's Protection Against the Enemy

Psalm 91 is my favorite scripture on God's protection. I have memorized and hidden it in my heart. I have it posted right in front of my bed, and I also have it displayed on a cabinet in my office, where I can see it from my desk. I read or quote Psalm 91 every day. In the mornings, at night, and sometimes in between. I declare it over myself and my family.

God has promised that when we dwell in His presence, we abide under His shadow, and we have nothing to fear because He sends His angels to take care of us; they guide us in all our ways. No plague comes near our dwelling. He also delivers us, sets us on high, honors us, and satisfies us with long life, showing us His salvation.

The key is to dwell in or stay in God's presence, not just visit Him for a few minutes in the mornings with a short prayer or Bible verse and then forget about Him for the rest of the day or remember Him only on Sundays and then forget about Him for the rest of the week. When we dwell in God's presence, we abide under the shadow of the Almighty, remaining under His protection. No plague or sickness comes near our dwelling, for His wings shield us, and His angels keep us safe. When we leave God's presence, we expose ourselves to the enemy because His covering—His feathers—are not over us.

Start your day with God and end it with God—at home, in the car, at work or school, in church, and everywhere. Talk to Him in the morning, during the day, and have a conversation through prayer before you sleep. You don't have to be on your knees before you talk to God. In your home, you can get on your knees if that is what you are led to do, but you can talk to God anywhere. This takes practice and effort, but remember that you can do all things through Christ Jesus who strengthens you (see Philippians 4:13).

Try to make it your habit to read your Bible every day, take a verse or verses for meditation, and keep your mind focused on God's promises for your life and healing. Declare those promises over your life. Joshua 1:8 tells us that God's Word should not depart from our mouth, but we should meditate on it day and night. I suggest you write a verse or two on stick-it pads and post it where you will see it or write in a small notebook where you can look at it as often as you can during the day, or better still, you could screenshot your verse of the day on your phone and, whenever you can, take five minutes or more to just read and meditate on it—mutter it to yourself, focus on it and allow it sink into your spirit. This will help you keep your mind on God's promises for your life and healing and equip you to *"cast down arguments and every high thing that exalts itself against the knowledge of God, bringing every thought into captivity to the obedience of Christ." (2 Corinthians 10:5 – NKJV)*. The enemy uses your thoughts and imagination to instill fear and unbelief. You begin to doubt whether God's Word is true or not, or even if it is true, whether it will work for you or not.

FAITH IN CHRIST OVER FEAR OF CANCER

You need the Word of God—the double-edged sword—to cast down everything that contradicts God's promises and continue to trust Him and remain under His protection.

There are many Bible apps available online, in case you prefer that. I use both my physical hard copy Bible and the Bible app. You cannot grow in your faith and remain in God's presence if you don't spend time with Him. Have scriptures you can meditate on, and keep speaking those scriptures over your life. Entrust Him with your life! Know that He will not let the devil overcome you, as long as you remain in His presence. He will protect you. But if you leave His presence, you become vulnerable to the enemy. Satan's goal is to steal, kill, and destroy. If he can convince you to doubt God, he can get you to leave God's presence and protection, which will give him access to your soul (mind, will, and emotions) and body.

We are told in 1 Peter 5:8 to be sober-minded and watchful because our adversary, the devil, prowls around like a roaring lion, seeking whom he may devour. When you dwell in God's presence, the enemy cannot devour you. Jesus already defeated the devil. Have faith that God is protecting you. No matter what happens around you or how your body feels, believe that He will satisfy you with a long life and show you His salvation (see Psalm 91:16).

Chapter 7

Fear Not, The Lord Is With You

> *"But now, thus says the Lord, who created you, O Jacob, and He who formed you, O Israel: "Fear not, for I have redeemed you; I have called you by your name; You are Mine. When you pass through the waters, I will be with you; and through the rivers, they shall not overflow you. When you walk through the fire, you shall not be burned, nor shall the flame scorch you." (Isaiah 43:1-2 – NKJV).*

Fear is a weapon the enemy uses to keep us from experiencing God's promises and purpose for our lives. Fear is a spirit that torments us and causes us to lose our peace and faith in God. According to 1 John 4:18, *"There is no fear in love; but perfect love cast out fear, because fear involves torment. But he who fears has not been made perfect in love." (NKJV).* Fear is one of our greatest enemies, so we must constantly prepare ourselves to battle the spirit of fear. Fear is always whispering something negative in our ears, telling us to walk by sight and not by faith, telling us that our prayers are either unanswered or unheard, telling us that God has abandoned us and we are alone, telling us to worry and not trust God, telling us that cancer and other diseases are bigger than God and so on. We all struggle with the spirit of fear. Whenever you feel afraid, turn to God in prayer.

In 2 Chronicles 20, when the great multitude of army came against the children of Judah, look at what the king did when he was afraid. *"And Jehoshaphat feared; and set himself to seek the Lord and proclaimed a fast throughout Judah." (2 Chronicles 20:3 - KJV)*. He set himself to **seek the Lord**. Seek the Lord, and He will help you face and defeat the spirit of fear. When you rely on Him, He will fight for you as He did for the children of Judah. God is no respecter of persons; we are Abraham's seed and heirs of the promise through Jesus Christ (see Galatians 3:14).

Before I began chemotherapy, I was afraid. However, I had a prayer group, which consisted of my sister, aunt, a friend who is our prayer partner, and me. We prayed and sought God's guidance. My husband and I also prayed together. After a few days of prayer, my friend and prayer partner called and told me that the Lord had said that I should not be afraid and that chemotherapy would help me and not harm me. That gave me assurance, and I went ahead with chemotherapy. It wasn't easy, but I held on to God's Word and cast out fear with prayer and faith, because I knew the Lord was with me. And true to His Word, God was with me throughout my treatment.

I was strong and remained joyful, and the doctors and nurses always said that I looked "bright," and they were surprised at how I remained that way throughout my treatment. I told them that the Lord was with me; He gave me strength.

Several weeks into chemo, I needed a blood transfusion. I had never had a blood transfusion in my life, so I became afraid. Again, the Lord spoke through the Holy Spirit and encouraged me not to be afraid; He was with me. So, whenever I went for a blood transfusion, I spoke over the blood. I declared that it was transformed into the blood of Jesus and that nothing was going to go wrong. While the blood was being transfused into my body, I kept on declaring God's Word and thanking the Lord that this was His blood, and it was flushing away all cancer cells from my body. I did not shout, but I muttered the words under my breath, and I always had healing scriptures or praise and worship music playing in my ears as I received chemotherapy and blood transfusion. God came through for me, and everything went as planned. I did experience hair loss and a few other symptoms, but there was no damage to my organs, and not once was I admitted to the hospital. I walked in and out of that hospital every time I went for my treatment.

After chemotherapy, I was scheduled for surgery. Again, the devil tried to torment me with fear and "what ifs." However, I sought the Lord, and He led me to Isaiah 43:1-2. I read and meditated on this scripture until it sank into my spirit, and fear was cast out. I included my name and said:

> *"But now, thus says the Lord, who created you, O Jestina, and He who formed you, O Neejay (my middle name): Fear not, for the Lord has redeemed you; He has called you by name, you are His. When you passed through the waters of chemotherapy, He was with you; He will be with you through surgery; the rivers shall not overflow you. When you walk through the fire of radiation, you shall not be burned, nor shall the flame scorch you. There will be no side effects because the Lord is with you. Fear not, Jestina, God's got you!"*

I believed every word, and I did not drown, nor did I get burned.

Believing God's Word and trusting His perfect love for me subdued my fears. I went for surgery, knowing that God had already gone ahead of me. The surgery was successful, and I was discharged two days after my breast surgery. Glory to God! I am a living testimony that God's Word is alive and powerful, and all the promises of God in Him (Jesus Christ) are Yes and Amen, to the glory of God (see 2 Corinthians 1:20).

I don't know the journey you, or maybe a loved one, is going through right now, but I do know that God loves you, and He will come through for you, or your loved one, if you rely on Him.

FAITH IN CHRIST OVER FEAR OF CANCER

I have shared some of my journey through fear and how trusting in God helped me overcome it. So, I know from experience that the devil attacks us with fear so we can doubt God's love and give him room to torment us. When we trust in God's unfailing love for us, He gives us the courage to overcome fear so that we are not controlled by it. Fear will always be around because our adversary, the devil, walks about like a roaring lion, seeking whom he may devour (see 1 Peter 5:8). That is why we need to be alert to the tricks of the devil and conscious of God's love.

During my early childhood, my father would sometimes go out of town for work and stay away for a few days or even a few weeks, but he always returned. However, when I was about seven years old, he left, and I thought he had gone on one of his trips, as he often did, and would come back. But this time, he didn't return. I remember sitting on the stairs at the front of the house, looking out for him as the days turned into weeks, the weeks into months, and then the months turned into years. One day, when I was about nine or ten years old, as I sat thinking about where my father was and why he had left us, I started to pray. Although I knew God existed and we prayed in our home, I didn't have a personal relationship with Him, but I wanted my father back. I remember telling God that my father had left, and I needed a father, so I needed Him to be my father. Later that evening, I lay on the bed and began to cry as I asked God to take over the role of my father. After crying my heart out, I said, *"God, I need a hug. Can you hug me, please?"* In that moment, I felt a warmth and a calm come over me. I felt joy and a sense of peace. And from that day, I did not grieve over my father again. I believed that God loved me more than he did, and God would never leave me. Even though I couldn't see God, I could feel His presence. And since that day, I have always trusted in God's love for me.

My father eventually came back after several years, but God took care of me and my family when he left, so since then, I have always depended on God to supply my needs and protect me. That is why when the devil attacked my health and life with breast cancer, I turned to my heavenly Father for help. His love and grace have carried me through many trying times, and I knew He would come through for me. Yes, there was fear, but trusting in God's love and remembering all the times He came through for me helped me face it, knowing that nothing can separate me from the love of God, which is in Christ Jesus, our Lord (see Romans 8:38-39). I spent a lot of time in His presence, reading and meditating on healing scriptures. The more time I spent in the Word, the more real His love for me became.

You may be going through cancer or a terminal disease or a lack in some area of your life because you have seen the doctor's report, or you are not feeling well in your body, and the spirit of fear is attacking you and telling you that you are not going to make it. When we are going through challenging times, Satan tries to make us doubt God's love by telling us that if God loved us, we wouldn't be going through sickness or pain or lack. But he is the one who is attacking us, and we need to know that the devil is the enemy and the oppressor, and he is still attacking us with fear and doubt to prevent us from enjoying the good health, long life, and prosperity that Jesus bought with His own blood for us. Don't buy into that lie. Jesus loves us so much that while we were in sin, He died for us.

Romans 5:8 tells us, *"But God demonstrates His own love toward us, in that while we were still sinners, Christ died for us." (NKJV)*. I urge you to trust that God's love will carry you through this season of your life. You may feel like hope is gone, but that isn't the case. God loves you and cares for you. He is with you. He will never leave you nor forsake you. He was with me and brought me through stage three, triple negative invasive breast cancer, and today, I am alive and testifying of His love and healing power in my life. God is for you, and He is with you and fighting for you.

Don't allow the enemy to control you with fear. God is your healer. In Jeremiah 30:17, He promised to restore your health and heal your wounds, and He will. Fear not; only believe! Weeping may endure for a night, but joy comes in the morning. Stand firm, beloved. Your joy is on the way.

In Daniel 3 and 6, Shadrach, Meshach, and Abednego were thrown into the fire, but they did not get burned because God sent His angel to deliver them. Daniel was thrown into the lion's den, but he came out unscathed; the Lord saved him. The same God who saved them is your healer, and He will deliver you from cancer and any disease or obstacle. Those who put their trust in Him will never be put to shame. His eyes run to and fro throughout the whole earth to show Himself strong on behalf of those who fear Him (see 2 Chronicles 16:9). God has already made provision for your healing through Jesus Christ. Fear not; only believe. God is for you, and He is with you!

Chapter 8

Stand Firm

> *"Therefore, take up the whole armor of God, that you may be able to withstand the evil day, and having done all, to stand." (Ephesians 6:13 – NKJV).*

Breast cancer was "the evil day" I went through. From the time I was diagnosed to the time I was declared cancer-free was sixteen months. Those were the longest months of my life and a true test of my faith in God. However, I am grateful to God because during those months, I came to know Jesus as my healer, and my life and relationship with God have grown to a whole new level. When we feed on God's Word and remain connected to Him through prayers, Jesus becomes our firm foundation, and He strengthens us to put on the whole armor of God through faith.

The Holy Spirit helps us stand firm despite the negative medical reports or symptoms we may be facing. I do not know "the evil day" you are going through right now, but I know that Jesus can take you through if you have faith in Him and believe His Word concerning your healing. Fear shakes our faith and causes us to take our eyes off Jesus and focus on the wind and waves (medical report, our body, our feelings). When we take our eyes off Jesus, as Peter did, our faith starts to waver, and we begin to sink. But our God is merciful, and whenever we cry out to Him, as Peter did, and say, "Lord, save me," Jesus reaches out His hand and saves us.

When I was diagnosed with breast cancer, I prayed for healing. I continued to read my Bible, pray, and declare God's Word concerning healing. But the more I prayed and declared, the lump grew bigger. Fear started to torment me. But every time fear rose up, I prayed and countered it with the Word of God. I told the devil that he is a liar and that I was healed because God says I am healed, and God cannot lie. It wasn't always easy, but I kept my eyes on Jesus by praying, listening to healing messages, and reading and declaring healing scriptures while going through my treatment until I eventually became cancer-free.

What does it mean to stand firm? To stand firm means to remain unshaken and unmoved by your surroundings, what you see, your feelings, your symptoms, or the medical report, and instead keep your position, standing with your eyes and heart fixed on Jesus Christ, the solid rock, the Word of God, the foundation of your faith, your healer and provider.

FAITH IN CHRIST OVER FEAR OF CANCER

How can you stand firm when the storms are raging, and hope seems lost? According to Ephesians 6:11, to stand firm, you need to *"Put on the whole armor of God, that you may be able to stand against the wiles of the devil." (NKJV)*. Wiles refers to the tactics or deceptions employed by the enemy. The devil has come to steal, kill, and destroy. He tries to trick us into believing that we are not healed or that we do not deserve to be healed. The Bible tells us that *"we have been saved by grace through faith" (see Ephesians 2:8),* so we can never work hard enough to be righteous or earn God's blessings, which include healing. Jesus already did all the work for us. We must believe and receive. If someone hands you a gift, you must reach out and take it before it become yours, even though the person already bought it for you and may have printed your name on it. Jesus has redeemed us from the curse of the law (see Galatians 3:13), and our redemption includes salvation, healing, peace, and every good and perfect gift. We just need to reach out and accept the gift of healing that Jesus gave His life for, just as we accepted Him as our Lord and Savior.

I know that it is sometimes hard to accept that you are healed when you are still seeing and feeling symptoms and pain in your body. The enemy never gets tired of whispering negative thoughts in your head, which leads to fear, anxiety, unbelief, and so on. This is a constant battle, so we must stand firm and not give in to fear, unbelief, discouragement, etc., or give up on God's promises for our healing. We must ask the Holy Spirit to help us walk in the spirit. This is a journey I am currently on, seeking the Holy Spirit and asking

Him to lead me in every area of my life. The Bible says in Romans 8:14-15, *"For as many as are led by the Spirit of God these are sons of God. For you did not receive the spirit of bandage again to fear, but you received the spirit of adoption by whom we cry out, 'Abba Father."* (NKJV). When we walk in the spirit, we will not gratify the desires of the flesh. For me, that includes not allowing my body (flesh) to tell me I am not healed; instead, I walk in the spirit and believe that I am healed, according to God's Word.

To stand firm, we must wear the whole armor of God as we prepare for battle each day. Our enemy, the devil, doesn't stop attacking, so we should keep in mind that this is an ongoing battle. We must be sober and vigilant. Remember that you are putting on the armor of God, and when we wear God's armor, we have God's army backing us. Before preparing for the battle, we need to know our enemy. Who are we fighting? Ephesians 6:12 tells us that we are not wrestling against flesh and blood; our battle is not with physical opponents. Instead, we are fighting against the rulers, against the authorities, against the powers of the dark world, and against spiritual forces of evil in the heavenly realms. Disease and afflictions are the oppression of the devil.

I believe that cancer is an evil spirit that is fed and strengthened by the spirit of fear. Because the battle is spiritual, we must prepare God's way. God is a Spirit (see John 4:24). His army is not a human army, so even though we may not see them, they are still fighting with us. In 2

Kings 6:8-18, the King of Syria sent his army, and they surrounded the city where the prophet Elisha was with the intent of capturing him because all of his war plans against Israel, made behind closed doors, were revealed to Elisha by God, and Elisha, in turn, informed the king of Israel. When Elisha's servant saw that they were surrounded by the army with horses and chariots, he became afraid. He knew that they could not escape such an army. What he didn't know was that God had sent an army larger and mightier than the Syrian army. Even though Elisha's servant could not see them physically, God's army of horses and chariots of fire was already in position, ready to fight. Elisha prayed and asked God to open the eyes of his servant. God opened his eyes, and he saw the army of the Lord. The Syrian army did not stand a chance! The Bible tells us in Psalm 34:7 that, *"The angel of the Lord encamps all around those who fear Him, and delivers them." (NKJV)*. Angels are all around you to deliver you.

As you put on the whole armor of God and prepare for battle, know that God's army is already in position. You are not alone. And after you have done all to stand, keep standing firm and don't give up or give in. Victory is yours because you are more than a conqueror through Jesus Christ who loves you. You will win the battle because the Lord is backing you, so no matter how long the battle may last, victory is certain with the Lord.

Let's get ready for battle: *"Stand therefore, having girded your waist with **truth**, having put on the **breastplate of***

***righteousness**, and having shod your feet with the **preparation of the gospel of peace;** above all, taking on the **shield of faith** with which you will be able to quench all the fiery darts of the wicked one. And take the **helmet of salvation**, and the **sword of the spirit**, which is the word of God; **praying always with all prayer and supplication in the Spirit**, being watchful to this end with all perseverance and supplication for all the saints." (Ephesians 6:14-18 – NKJV - emphasis mine).* You must put on or wear the armor of God. You dress up daily for the battle.

Having girded your waist with truth: The belt is tied around the waist of the soldier to keep the breastplate secure and in place. What truth do you need to gird your waist with? The truth of God's Word. John 8:32 tells us, *"And you shall know the truth, and the truth shall make you free." (NKJV).* The truth of God's Word keeps all other pieces of the armor in place. Without it, your armor will not remain stable, which may leave a gap for the enemy to have access to you. Know the truth that is written in the Bible: what God says regarding the situation you are facing, not the report given by the doctor or your body. What do I mean? Yes, the doctor may have seen a tumor, cancer cells, or some disease; yes, your body may be hurting or feeling weak, but that is not God's truth concerning your health and life. God's truth is that by the stripes of Jesus Christ, you were healed, and so sickness has no place in your body. It is an oppression of the devil, and it must leave your body in Jesus' name. God's truth is that He will restore you to health and heal your wounds (see Jeremiah 30:17). God's truth is that Jesus Himself took your infirmities and bore your sicknesses, so you don't have to bear cancer or any disease in your body (see Matthew 8:17). Hold on to the truth of God's Word. Gird your waist with the truth of God's Word as you go into battle each day so that the truth of God's Word will become your truth and prevail over any report that contradicts God's truth.

Having put on the breastplate of righteousness: The breastplate covers the soldier's shoulders, chest, and back and protects the vital organs, including the heart, from attack. The breastplate is held in place by the belt on the waist (gird your waist with truth). I would say the modern-day breastplate is akin to a bulletproof jacket. We protect our heart and other vital spiritual organs from the bullets of the devil by putting on the righteousness of Christ.

Remember that we are putting on the armor of God; therefore, we put on the righteousness of Jesus, not our own righteousness. 2 Corinthians 5:21 tells us, *"For He made Him who knew no sin to be sin for us, that we might become the righteousness of God in Him." (NKJV).* We cannot withstand the attacks of the enemy through self-righteousness or good works because the Bible says in Isaiah 64:6 that *"all our righteousness are as filthy rags." (KJV).* We cannot cleanse our sins by good deeds; only the blood of Jesus can do that for us. When we repent of our sins and accept Jesus as our Lord and Savior, His blood cleanses us from all unrighteousness.

The breastplate of righteousness also protects our heart. The Bible tells us in Proverbs 4:23 to *"Keep your heart with all diligence, for out of it spring the issues of life." (NKJV)*. The righteousness we have through Jesus Christ gives us the right to divine health and healing, long life and prosperity, and abundant life. Therefore, when the devil tells you that you do not deserve to be healed or God is punishing you with sickness, you rebuke him with the Word of God and declare that you are under the covering of the righteousness of Jesus, not your own righteousness, because as it is written in 1 Peter 2:24 that Jesus Christ Himself took your sin in His own body on the tree, that you having died to sin might live for righteousness; by His stripes you have been healed. Stand firm and put on the breastplate of righteousness each day. Spend time reading the Bible and praying so that you can abide in God's presence so the Holy Spirit can guide you daily.

We are to "put on" the breastplate of righteousness daily for battle. We must dedicate our lives and daily activities to God and ask the Holy Spirit to guide us and help us live according to the Word, resisting temptation so that the devil may flee from us. When we draw near to God, He also draws near to us (see James 4:8). We have hope in the salvation that God has given us through Jesus, and this hope keeps our faith alive in our hearts.

> *"For with the heart one believes unto righteousness, and with the mouth confession is made unto salvation."*
> *(Romans 10:10 – NKJV).*

FAITH IN CHRIST OVER FEAR OF CANCER

When the Word of God guides us, the truth of God's Word keeps our breastplate of righteousness in place so that we are fully protected from the attacks of the enemy.

Having your feet shod with the preparation of the gospel of peace: We must walk in obedience to God's Word. We are all sinners, but we should not deliberately remain in sin. When you sin, confess your wrongdoing and ask God to help you forsake those sinful habits and actions. We can only do that when our feet are firmly planted in the gospel, and we surrender to Jesus, so that He can give us peace that surpasses all human understanding.

When I was diagnosed, my husband could not understand why I was so calm. He kept saying, *"You're very strong."* I always responded that God is my strength. One of the things the devil tries to take away from us through sickness is our peace. We become fearful and anxious, and that causes more harm to us. Peace is part of the atonement Jesus made through His death on the cross because the **"chastisement of our peace was upon Him" (Isaiah 53:5).** This verse always helps to calm me and gives me assurance when I begin to feel anxious.

When we keep our minds on Jesus, He will keep us in perfect peace (see Isaiah 26:3). Jesus Himself is our peace; that is why when He was in the boat with His disciples, as they were panicking and crying out because of the heavy storm that was raging all around them and the boat was covered with waves, Jesus was in the same boat, unmoved, unbothered and so calm that He was sleeping during the heavy storm. His disciples had to wake Him up. When He got up, Jesus didn't panic or become anxious. *"Then He arose and rebuked the wind, and said to the sea, 'Peace, be still!' And the wind ceased and there was a great calm." (Mark 4:39).* Jesus has already been chastised for our peace. He is in the "boat" of sickness and affliction with you. Don't let fear steal your peace; Jesus is your peace. Shod your feet, stand grounded with the gospel—the good news—of healing and abundant life that Jesus purchased for us with His own blood, and allow the peace of God to guide your heart and mind. Speak to that storm (sickness/obstacles) in your life and declare, *"Peace be still, in Jesus' name."*

Above all, taking on the shield of faith with which you will be able to quench all the fiery darts of the wicked one: the foundation of the Christian life is faith. I have not seen God physically, nor have you, but through faith, we believe He exists. The same faith you applied, with the help of the Holy Spirit, to believe that God exists and Jesus died to give you salvation and eternal life, is the same faith you need to quench all the fiery arrows of the devil.

Faith is our shield from all the attacks of the enemy. In battles, a shield is used to intercept or block attacks and protect the soldier. It can also be used as an offensive weapon to strike the enemy. Faith in Jesus is our shield during the battle against the enemy, both to block and put out all the fiery arrows and also launch counterattacks by keeping faith alive by hearing, believing, and declaring God's Word every day. Meditate on the Word and counter every arrow by sending it back to the sender, in Jesus' name.

"Have faith in God," Jesus told His disciples after He cursed the fig tree, and they saw later that it had withered just as Jesus had said (see Mark 11:21-22). Jesus is saying to you, *"Have faith in God."* Faith is the substance of things (healing/breakthrough, etc.) hoped for and the evidence of things not seen. The Word of God is the evidence of what we have not seen. We believe, and eventually, we will see.

And take the helmet of salvation: In battle, the helmet protects the soldier's head—the helmet protects the head and mind. Put on the helmet of salvation by keeping your thoughts on Jesus and His promises for your health and healing. Keep your mind on the Word of God so you don't fall into the enemy's deceptions.

The battles (doubts, fear, anxiety, etc.) start within your mind, so you must fill it with the Word of God to counter all negative thoughts. You cannot keep the Word in mind if you don't read and study the Bible. The Word will save your health and your life; it is your salvation. When you set aside time every day to read the Bible, you will see that God is a good God, He loves you, and He wants you well. Believe that He is your heavenly Father, and He sent His only begotten Son to die for you and me, so that we can enjoy abundant life here on earth, NOW, not tomorrow, and not only in heaven. Pray that His will be done in your life on earth as it is in heaven. There is no sickness in heaven! Keep your mind and thoughts focused on Jesus, your Savior, not on the disease or obstacle.

And the sword of the spirit, which is the word of God: "For the word of God is living and powerful, and sharper than any two-edged sword, piercing even to the dividing of soul and spirit, and of joints and marrow, and is a discerner of the thoughts and intents of the heart." (Hebrews 4:12 – NKJV). The Word of God is sharper than any two-edged sword; it can cut cancer and all disease from the root and shred it to pieces.

The Bible tells us that God created man and all things in heaven and earth through His Word. He has given us His Word—the Bible—to create life or death; that power is in our mouths. Use God's written Word to execute vengeance on all disease and setbacks (see Psalm 149:6, 9). Confess healing scriptures over your life, morning, afternoon, evening, and anywhere in between. Be intentional because you are on the battlefield, and your enemy, the devil, will not relent. So don't get weary. Jesus is your strength. You can do all things through Christ Jesus who strengthens you. Keep speaking the Word.

God's Word will never return to Him void; it will accomplish what is written. You need to keep declaring it, and God will hasten His Word to bring it to pass. He can't act if you don't speak. Speak to the mountain, in the name of Jesus, and it will give way if you believe. For me, I speak life and healing over my life and my family every day. I have healing scriptures right in front of my bed. I read them aloud every morning, declare them as often as I can during the day, and read them again before going to bed. It is a habit that I have developed, and I will continue to practice for the rest of my life, by God's grace. As pastor says, *"A closed mouth is a closed destiny."* If God had not spoken, you and I would not have been created. But He did speak, and here we are. So, speak in line with God's Word and see your healing manifest. Jesus gave us an example of how to speak the Word during His temptation in the wilderness. To every temptation, He responded, "It is written" (see Matthew 4:4-11).

Praying always with prayer in the Spirit, being watchful to this end with all perseverance and supplication for all the saints: The battle is fought on our knees in prayer. Prayer is the bridge that God has given us on earth to connect and reach Him in heaven. This battle is spiritual, so we must remember that we need to *"Pray without ceasing." (1 Thessalonians 5:17 - KJV).* When we pray, we invite God to act on our behalf. And when we pray, we do not give up. We stand firm and persevere until we see our breakthrough. We remain firm in prayer, continually calling on God and believing that He hears us and is with us. For me, I kept prayer alarms on my phone, set for 6:30 am and 8:00 am, and I joined the prayer line from my current location. I also set alarms for 3:00 pm and 7:00 pm, and then again before going to sleep. I did not have a set duration for prayer, but I had my aunt with me, and we prayed together at 3:00 p.m. and 7:00 p.m.

Do what works for you, but be intentional about praying if you want to see your breakthrough. Even after you are healed, keep your prayer life active so that your bridge to God remains in place.

Chapter 9

Praise Is Our Weapon For Victory

"Let the peoples praise you, o God; let the peoples praise You. Then the earth shall yield her increase; God, our own God, shall bless us." (Psalm 67:5-6 – NKJV).

Praise the Lord! When we praise God, He blesses us. The Lord inhabits the praises of His people. Praise is where God lives. Praise lets God know that you trust Him to fight for you. When you praise God, even when you have not seen the evidence, you are letting the devil know that your God is bigger than any trial that comes your way. And when you declare that you trust God and have faith in Him through your praise and worship, He fights your battles for you.

I believe that David was a man after God's own heart because David was a man of praise. He said in Psalm 34:1, *"I will bless the Lord at all times: his praise shall continually be in my mouth." (KJV).* Psalms 150:6 says, *"Let everything that has breath praise the Lord. Praise the*

Lord!" (NKJV). Do you have breath? Yes, you do! So, you need to begin to praise God right now. Praise Him for the battles He has won for you. Praise Him for being with you right now, and praise Him for defeating the battle of cancer and all diseases that may come your way.

There are several instances in the Bible where God delivered His people as they praised Him. Let's look at a few, beginning with Joshua 9, which tells the story of the wall of Jericho. This is a familiar story, but let's observe what happened before the wall fell.

> *"And the Lord said to Joshua: "See! I have given Jericho into your hand, its king, and the mighty men of valor." (Joshua 6:2 – NKJV).*

The Lord went on to give Joshua instructions about how they were to march around the wall of Jericho. Notice that God said He had given them Jericho, even though they had not yet begun the march around the wall and had not actually taken over Jericho physically. Yet, Joshua believed God's Word and obeyed His instructions. The children of Israel marched around the wall one time for six days. On the seventh day, they marched around the wall seven times, and the priest blew the trumpets. According to Joshua 6:20, *"So the people shouted when the priests blew the trumpets. And it happened when the people heard the sound of the trumpet, and the people shouted with a great shout, that the wall fell down flat. Then the people went up into the city, every man straight before him, and they took the city." (NKJV).*

What if Joshua had not believed God's Word and obeyed His instructions, and the children of Israel had not given that shout of praise and victory before seeing the evidence? I do not think the walls would have fallen, and they would not have taken over the city, even though God had already made victory available to them. However, they believed and obeyed God, and their praise became a weapon that brought down the walls of Jericho.

Will you begin to praise God right now for your healing and deliverance so that walls of affliction and sickness can fall down flat? He has already given you His Word concerning your healing (see Isaiah 53:4-5, 1 Peter 2:24, Galatians 3:13, Exodus 15:26). Have faith in God and begin to praise Him for making healing available to you. Praise will tell the devil that he has nothing on you because you believe in God's Word, and victory is yours in Jesus' name.

Another story is that of Jehoshaphat, King of Judah. In 2 Chronicles 20, we see that three nations joined forces to attack Judah. Jehoshaphat knew that he could not fight them with his own strength, so he turned to the Lord for help. He called a fast throughout Judah, and they prayed to God for help. In 2 Chronicles 20:12, Jehoshaphat said, *"O our God, will You not judge them? For we have no power against this great multitude that is coming against us, nor do we know what to do, **but our eyes are upon you.**" (NKJV – emphasis mine)*. God heard and gave them His Word. He said, *"Do not be afraid nor be dismayed because of the great* *multitude, for the battle is not yours, but God's." (2* Chronicles 20:15b - NKJV*).*

On the day of the battle, *"he (Jehoshaphat) appointed those who should sing to the Lord, and those who should praise the beauty of holiness, as they went out before the army and were saying: 'Praise the Lord, for His mercy endures forever.'" (2 Chronicles 20:21 - NKJV).* 2 Chronicles 20:22 states, *"Now when they began to sing and to praise, the Lord set ambushes against the people of Ammon, Moab, and Mount Seir, who had come against Judah; and they were defeated." (NKJV).*

Isn't that incredible! As the children of Judah praised God, He fought for them and defeated their enemies. It didn't matter that they were outnumbered; it didn't matter that three nations joined forces against them, because the Almighty God was on their side. If God be for you, who can be against you? The children of Judah, led by King Jehoshaphat, trusted in God; they believed His Word and praised Him even before their enemies were defeated. They believed that God had already done it before they saw the evidence. God came through for them because He had given His Word, and it is impossible for God to lie or change His mind. He will do what He says.

You already know what is written concerning your healing. God has spoken to you through His Word. Will you believe and begin to praise your way to victory as King Jehoshaphat did? Or are you going to believe what the medical report or your body is saying? God is saying, *"Do not be dismayed at the great multitude (cancer, diabetes, high blood pressure, etc.), for the battle is not yours, it's the Lord's!"* Praise the Lord! The King of kings is fighting for you. Jesus has already won the battle for you. Rise up and begin to praise the Lord for your healing because you shall not die but live and declare the works of the Lord! Hallelujah!

One more evidence of the power of praise is displayed when Paul and Silas were imprisoned in Acts 16:25-26, which states, *"But at midnight Paul and Silas were praying and singing hymns to God, and the prisoners were listening to them. Suddenly there was a great earthquake, so that the foundations of the prison were shaken; and immediately all the doors were opened, and everyone's chains were loosed."* (NKJV).

Paul and Silas were imprisoned because Paul cast out the spirit of divination from a slave girl who had been making money for her owners. She had followed them for several days as they went for prayer, and Paul got annoyed, cast the spirit out of her in the name of Jesus, and the spirit came out of her immediately. Her owners, realizing that their hope of profit was gone, dragged Paul and Silas to the authorities, and they were put into prison.

While in prison, Paul and Silas did not sit and cry about their situation. They did not blame God for allowing them to be imprisoned. They did not allow the enemy to defeat them. They knew that their God was with them, and He was willing and able to deliver them. They did not sleep, nor did they grow weary. Instead of allowing the enemy to bring them down, they used the weapon that they knew would bring them victory. They began to pray and sing hymns! They praised and glorified God. They knew God had won many battles for them, and He was not about to leave them or forsake them. As they began to pray and praise, there was a great earthquake; the foundation of the prison was shaken; all the doors were opened, and their chains were loosed—not just them but all the prisoners.

Are you still silent? Are you still asking, "Why me?" Are you allowing the enemy to take what belongs to you? No way! Rise up and praise your God, the One who created you and formed you before you were in your mother's womb. I AM that I AM is your God. Jesus was made manifest that He might destroy all the works of Satan. Glory to God!

Go back to the times when God came through for you. Remember the times you called on Him and He made a way for you. Don't wait until you feel good or feel like praising. Begin to praise the Lord, and you will feel better. Remember that you walk by faith and not by sight. Faith says, *"Lord, I thank You that I am healed because You are the Lord who heals me."* Faith says, *"Jesus, I believe that You already took my infirmities and bore all my diseases, and I praise You that, according to 1 Peter 2:24, by Your stripes, I was healed."* Faith says, *"Lord, I praise You for restoring my health and healing my wounds, as is written in Jeremiah 30:17."* As long as you are breathing, you have a reason to praise the Lord. Praise is your weapon of victory; use it now and begin to praise the Lord.

Psalm 149:1 says, *"Praise the Lord! Sing to the Lord a new song, and His praise in the assembly of saints." (NKJV).* Psalm 103:1-3 states, *"Bless the Lord, O my soul; and all that is within me bless His holy name! Bless the Lord, O my soul, and forget not all His benefits. Who forgives all your iniquities, who heals all your diseases." (NKJV). Let everything that has breath praise the Lord. Praise the Lord! (Psalm 150: 6 – NKJV).*

Chapter 10

How To Keep Your Healing

"What do you conspire against the Lord? He will make an utter end of it. Affliction will not rise up a second time."
(Nahum 1:9 – NKJV).

In the same way you believed God for your healing, continue to trust that He has made an utter end of cancer and any other disease or affliction; it will not return to your body, for the blood of Jesus has destroyed it. Remember where God took you from; if He was able to heal you, He can also keep you in good health. Believe that your healing is permanent, and affliction will not rise up a second time.

Every day, I confess Nahum 1:9 because sometimes fear starts to rise the moment I experience a headache or a bit of fatigue. However, as soon as I hear that voice starting to raise negative thoughts and possibilities, I quench it with the Word of God. Remember where God has taken you from and trust that He will always keep you in good health, according to His Word. Keep your faith active and alive by reading the Bible daily and nourishing your faith with healing scriptures so that you can continue to hold on to God's promises of good health and long life.

During my healing journey, I listened to numerous messages on healing, and one of them was "Healing Scriptures" with Mrs. Dodie Osteen. In her YouTube video, Mrs. Dodie gives her testimony of how the Lord healed her supernaturally of metastatic liver cancer when she was in her forties. She said that the cancer had spread, and the doctors gave her two weeks to live. She and her husband, their church, and so many others prayed and believed God for her healing, and she was healed. After her healing, she made the video over thirty years after her healing, and cancer had never returned since her healing.

According to Mrs. Osteen, when she was given two weeks to live by the doctors, instead of giving up, she prayed for other people and read several healing scriptures every day. Even after her healing, she continues to read those healing scriptures every single day, which she believes have made it possible for her to maintain her healing. She doesn't leave her house without reading her healing scriptures daily, and she was healed of cancer for more than thirty-five years at the time of the YouTube video. Cancer has never returned, and it will never return because the Lord has made an utter end of cancer, according to Nahum 2:9.

FAITH IN CHRIST OVER FEAR OF CANCER

Pastor Oral Roberts advised in His book, "Deliverance From Fear and Sickness" that to keep your healing, you should make up your mind that you are going to live a Christian life regardless of what happens to you; think positive thoughts and never allow your mind to entertain negative thoughts; and in times of discouragement or loneliness, you should read your Bible constantly, and keep your eyes on Jesus—that is the secret. Always keep your eyes on Jesus.

Keep your healing by remaining in fellowship with God. Don't return to wrong thinking and living because you are now healed. You have to remain in the *"shadow of the Almighty"* so He can continue to protect you. Remember that our adversary, the devil, is moving about like a roaring lion seeking to devour anyone whom the Lord does not protect. We must make the Bible our daily bread; we need to eat it daily to nourish our spirit, soul, and body.

What did you do when you needed your healing? Don't stop reading the Bible, listening to healing messages, praying, and declaring the Word of God. It is the written word that will keep your healing in your body, as you keep it before your eyes, in the midst of your heart, and in your mouth by confessing healing scriptures every day, even after you see your healing in your body. As for me, I still have my healing scriptures posted right in front of my bed. As soon as I wake up, I begin thanking and praising God for life and healing before adding other supplications. I declare Psalm 91 and Psalm 118:17 over my life and my family every day, and I also read several healing scriptures.

Decide to continue living for God and trust Him, no matter what you may face. I remember there were times during my healing journey when I felt discouraged, and the devil would taunt me that maybe God wasn't listening to me or maybe my faith wasn't strong enough for me to receive my healing and so on, and I would cry out to God that I needed Him to come through for me speedily. Why was my healing delayed from manifesting? But then the Holy Spirit reminded me of John 6:67-68. After Jesus had preached a message, most of His disciples had left Him. *"Then Jesus said to the twelve, 'Do you also want to go away?' But Simon Peter answered Him, 'Lord, to whom shall we go? You have the words of eternal life.'" (NKJV)*. This scripture reminded me that Jesus is the only one who can give me an abundant life here on earth and eternal life in heaven. So, to whom shall I go? And to whom shall you go, if not to Jesus? He is the one who gave His life for our health, healing, and long, abundant life. He is my help and salvation. I have no one to turn to but Him, as Peter said. Keep in the Lord's presence.

Start your day with God through prayer and scripture reading, and end it with God. Psalm 92:1-2 says, *"It is good to give thanks to the Lord, and to sing praises to your name, O Most High; To declare your loving kindness in the morning, and your faithfulness every night." (NKJV)*. Continue to dwell or live in the secret place of the Highest, and no evil will happen to you.

Associate with believers and people who will help build your faith. It could be your church, a prayer group, Bible-believing friends, etc. Try as much as you can to be connected to Christians who will help to keep your faith strong. I am on the NSPPD prayer altar, and I join every weekday, which helps build my faith and strengthens my prayer life.

Keep your mind renewed with God's promises for your healing; think positive thoughts. There is a saying that *"an idle mind is the devil's workshop."* Don't leave your mind empty or idle. Keep it filled with God's Word. Continue reading the Bible and filling your thoughts with God's promises for your health and healing. Think positive thoughts and cast down every thought and imagination that is contrary to the Word of God. When a negative thought starts to arise, and you start getting afraid that cancer or whatever disease you had before may return, rebuke that thought and begin to declare that *"by His stripes, you were healed."* Say to yourself that Jehovah Rapha is the Lord your healer; He wants you well.

> *"For the Son of Man did not come to destroy men's lives but to save them." (Luke 9:56 – NKJV).*

Keep your thoughts on the written Word of God. Anything that wants to steal, kill, or destroy you is not from God. Stand on your authority and continue to keep sickness away by standing your ground through faith.

Memorize scriptures and meditate on them to replace every negative thought of sickness and fear with positive thoughts. Affliction will not rise up a second time, in Jesus' name.

Whenever you feel discouraged, read the Bible. Find scriptures that give you strength and courage. Just Google it, and you will see several of them. Take your Bible and read. The Word of God is alive and active; you will find strength in times of need. I have done this over and over, and I always find peace, joy, and strength in the Bible when I take the time to read and ask the Holy Spirit for help. He is our teacher. He is also the power of God that works in us to do the will of God (see Philippians 2:13). God gives life to our mortal bodies through His Spirit that dwells in us. You have the power of God—the Holy Spirit—inside of you. Your body is His temple, so sickness cannot return to it or remain in your body. Deuteronomy 31:8 assures us, *"And the Lord, He is the One who goes before you. He will be with you; He will not leave you nor forsake you; do not fear nor be dismayed." (NKJV).* Always remember that the Lord is for you, and He is with you. Healing is ours to enjoy as part of the abundant life Jesus has given to us.

Keep *"Looking unto Jesus, the author and finisher of our faith" (Hebrews 12:2 – KJV).* No matter what happens in your life or health, keep your eyes on Jesus.

Before I close, let me share another story with you. At some point in my healing journey, even though I had heard the voice of the Holy Spirit say that I was not going to die, I allowed fear to take over my faith in God's Word. I was so desperate for healing that I began to search online for other alternatives. I felt the Word of God was too slow, so I downloaded some videos on how to use hypnotics for healing. As soon as I took the video to start playing, the Holy Spirit said, *"Don't. This is not of God. This will not bring glory to My name. I am the Lord, your healer. I told you that I've got you. Trust Me."*

I battled with these voices for a while—my flesh versus my spirit—and I tried to ignore the voice of the Holy Spirit, but thank God that I feared Him enough to resist the enemy's deception.

If I had gone through that for my healing, today, my life would have been completely different because I would not have relied on God for my healing. I would not have renewed my mind in the Word of God and in my relationship with God, and the glory would not have been given to God. I would not have had the opportunity to share God's healing and deliverance power and encourage those who may be going through similar journeys today. Thank God for His everlasting love and mercy. I am grateful!

Sometimes God takes His time with you. He takes you through a process because, at the end of the journey, you will be molded and polished, emerging as pure gold, ready to fulfill His purpose for your life. What the enemy meant for evil, God will change for your good. Trust Him! Do not be deceived by the enemy. All he wants is to steal from you:

your faith, health, relationships, finances, and, most of all, your life. Continue to nourish your faith and keep your eyes fixed on Jesus. He is in the boat with you, saying, *"Peace be still; fear not, My child; only believe."* Remember that God loves you, and He wishes, above all things, that you prosper and be in good health, even as your soul prospers. Keep believing, and you will remain healed and whole.

Healing Scriptures

Here are some of the healing scriptures I have quoted in this book. You can choose the ones that resonate with you and begin to meditate on them, confessing or declaring them over your life daily.

So then faith comes by hearing, and hearing by the word of God. (Romans 10:17 – NKJV).

For assuredly, I say to you, whoever says to this mountain (high blood pressure, diabetes, all pain, sickness, diseases and obstacles), 'Be removed and be cast into the sea,' and does not doubt in his heart, but believes that those things he say will be done, he will have whatever he says. (Mark 11:23 – NKJV - emphasis mine).

Therefore, I say to you, whatever things you ask for when you pray, believe that you receive them, and you will have them. (Mark 11:24 – NKJV).

For we walk by faith, not by sight. (2 Corinthians 5:7 – NKJV).

You will also declare a thing, and it shall be established for you; So light will shine on your ways. (Job 22:28 – NKJV).

Jesus Christ is the same yesterday, today and forever. (Hebrews 13:8 – NKJV).

Prayer/Declaration

Heavenly Father, as I read and declare these healing scriptures, I believe that Your Word will not return to You void but will accomplish what it says it will accomplish. Therefore, I believe in the name of Jesus that I am being healed as I read and declare the Word of God. I receive my healing, in Jesus' name. Amen.

I am the Lord that healeth thee. (Exodus 15:26 – KJV).

For I will restore health to you, and heal you of your wounds, says the Lord: (Jeremiah 30:17 – NKJV).

Who Himself bore our sins in His own body on the tree, that we, having died to sins, might live for righteousness - by whose stripes you were healed. (1 Peter 2:24 – NKJV).

Christ hath redeemed us from the curse of the law, having become a curse for us (for it is written, "Cursed is everyone who hangs on a tree." (Galatians 3:13 – NKJV).

I shall not die, but live, and declare the works of the Lord. (Psalm 118:17 – KJV).

Then Jesus went about all the cities and villages, teaching in their synagogues, preaching the gospel of the kingdom, and healing every sickness and every disease among the people. (Matthew 9:35 – NKJV).

At that very hour He cured many of infirmities, afflictions, and evil spirits, and to many blind He gave sight. (Luke 7:21 – NKJV).

Behold I will bring it health and healing; I will heal them and reveal to them the abundance of peace and truth. (Jeremiah 33:6 – NKJV).

Yet his days shall be one hundred and twenty years. (Genesis 6:3b – NKJV).

As your days, so shall your strength be. (Deuteronomy 33:25b – NKJV)

You shall come to your grave at a full age, as a sheaf of grain ripens in its season. (Job 5:26 – NKJV).

So you shall serve the Lord your God, and He shall bless your bread and your water. And I will take sickness from the midst of you. No one shall suffer miscarriage or be barren in your Land; I will fulfill the number of your days. (Exodus 23:25-26 – NKJV).

Oh Lord my God, I cried out to You and You healed me. O Lord, You brought my soul up from the grave; You have kept me alive, that I should not go down to the pit. (Psalm 30:2-3 – NKJV).

Our God is the God of salvation; and to God the Lord belong escapes from death. (Psalm 68:20 – NKJV).

Honor your father and mother, which is the first commandment with promise: "that it may be well with you and you may live long on the earth." (Ephesians 6:2-3 – NKJV).

Be anxious for nothing, but in everything by prayer and supplication, with thanksgiving, let your request be made known to God; and the peace of God, which surpasses all understanding will guard your hearts and minds through Christ Jesus. (Philippians 4:6-7 – NKJV).

Prayer/Declaration

Lord Jesus, I thank You for forgiving my sins and taking my sickness in Your own body on the cross. I give You glory for restoring my health and healing me of cancer (name the sickness, if not cancer) and every wound in my body. I believe that You have already taken my sins and sickness, so I do not have to carry them anymore. Thank You, Lord, for healing me of cancer (name the sickness, if not cancer) and every disease.

Thank You, Jesus, for redeeming me from the curse of the law, which includes all sickness and diseases. Thank You for becoming a curse for me so that I do not have to take the curse of sickness, including cancer, anymore. I believe that You are my healer, as it is written in Your Word. Therefore, I am healed in Jesus' name. You, spirit of cancer (and all diseases), in the name of Jesus Christ of Nazareth, I command you to leave my body now. Come out and never return, in Jesus' name. Amen.

Heavenly Father, I thank You for satisfying me with long life and showing me Your salvation. I stand in agreement with Your Word and declare that I shall not die but live and declare Your works. My days shall be long on the earth, and as my days, so shall my strength be, in Jesus' name. Amen.

Have faith in God, my sister or brother. God has already healed you. Fear not; only believe. Nothing is impossible with God. God bless you!

References

1. Hagen, K. E. (2010). *God's Medicine.* Electronic Edition. RHEMA Bible Church, AKA Kenneth Hagen Ministries, Inc.

2. Roberts O. (2018). *Deliverance From Fear and Sickness.* Electronic Edition. Muriwai Books.

3. Kennedy S. G. (2017). *The Simplicity of Healing. A Practical Guide to Releasing the Miracle Power of GOD's WORD.* Its Supernatural and Messianic Vision, Inc.

4. Hagen, K. E. (2010). *Healing Scriptures.* Electronic Edition. RHEMA Bible Church, AKA Kenneth Hagen Ministries, Inc.

5. Pastor Jerry Eze, OH LORD SHOW ME MERCY [MY CASE IS AN EMERGENCY] || NSPPD || 19TH October 2022 www.youtube.com/@PastorJerryEze

6. Pastor Jerry Eze, GLOBAL MID-YEAR FASTING & PRAYERS || DAY 6 || MY JOY IS FULL || NSPPD || 6TH JULY 2024 www.youtube.com/@PastorJerryEze

7. Sandra Kennedy, Your Healing is AS SIMPLE AS Getting Saved! | April 17, 2020
   www.youtube.com/@ISN-ItsSupernaturalNetwork

8. Dodie Osteen, Healing Scriptures w/Dodie Osteen | April Osteen Simons | February 2022
   www.youtube.com/@aprilosteensimons

9. Bible Study Tools (available at www.biblestudytools.com)

10. Bible Gateway (available at www.biblegateway.com)

www.ingramcontent.com/pod-product-compliance
Lightning Source LLC
Chambersburg PA
CBHW070504100426
42743CB00010B/1753